MADBOY

MAD**BOY**
MY JOURNEY FROM ADBOY TO ADMAN

RICHARD KIRSHENBAUM

OPEN **Ⓞ** ROAD
INTEGRATED MEDIA

NEW YORK

To Lucas,
From one madboy to another.
Do what you love and love what you do.
love,
Daddy

To Alterna-Dad,
To the original Mad Man.
A son could not have been luckier
to have a man like you as a father.

CONTENTS

INTRODUCTION

BY JERRY DELLA FEMINA

RICHARD KIRSHENBAUM ALMOST KILLED ME.

I was driving my car on New York's Henry Hudson Parkway on a rainy October morning in 1988 when I looked up and saw an outdoor billboard for Kenneth Cole shoes.

The headline, to get people to take part in the upcoming election, was just three letters: VOT.

The picture above it was George H.W. Bush's spelling-challenged Vice President, Dan Quayle.

The billboard was so funny, so fast, so perfect, I kept staring at it while I was driving 70 miles an hour, and I drifted into the next lane.

The driver whose car I had turned toward frantically honked his horn. I jammed on the brakes and my car skidded around and was now facing ongoing traffic.

Two cars driving behind me came within a whisker of slamming into me. I remember screaming out for my mother. When I finally turned the car in the right direction, I thought to myself, "I've got to meet the guy who wrote that poster."

Meeting Richie Kirshenbaum was love at first sight. He has the exuberance and the "please love me" energy of a puppy in a pet-shop window.

I once took Richie to the Four Seasons restaurant. It was his first time there. I gave him some big-brother advice.

"This is where you must come for lunch when you get a new account and it has been announced that morning in the *New York Times*, so all the important people in The Grill Room can see and celebrate with you."

Then I added, "This is where you must come on the day it is announced in the *New York Times* that you lost an account. That's to show the bastards you don't care."

During the course of our lunch, Richie told me the size of his new agency's billings three times.

Each time he told me a different number. Each number was lower than the last.

"He's starting to trust me," I thought.

❊   ❊   ❊   ❊

I would like to think Richie and I are very similar as advertising writers. We have humor and a "bad boy" shtick, and a "we're going to make you smile and charm you and all you have to do is look at our ad" mentality.

Once, many years ago, I went for a job at an agency called DeGarmo. The older man who was creative director called a friend of mine and screamed, "I will never hire him—he writes like an Italian street-corner wise guy."

He was right. My street corner was Avenue U and West 7th Street in Brooklyn.

I'm sure that if that same gentleman had seen Richie Kirshenbaum's copy portfolio 25 years later, he would have said, "I will never hire that guy—he writes like a Five Towns Jewish Long Island wise guy."

❊   ❊   ❊   ❊

The top three best-selling books on advertising can be summed up thusly:

In 1961, Rosser Reeves wrote a great book called *Reality in Advertising*. This was your basic "how advertising should be done" book.

In 1963, the great David Ogilvy wrote *Confessions of an Advertising Man*, which was basically a "how I did it" book.

In 1969, I wrote *From Those Wonderful Folks Who Gave You Pearl Harbor*. Since I hadn't yet done it and I didn't really know how to do it, my book was a "isn't advertising a fun thing to do for a living" book.

In 2011, with *Madboy*, Richie Kirshenbaum puts it all together in one great book on advertising. How it should be done. How he did it. And isn't it great fun.

Madboy is a terrific book, and I'm sure it will make an outstanding movie or television series.

Here's what I love about this book: If you're the parent of a teenager who's having problems at school and hints that he or she wants to do something "creative," buy him or her a copy of *Madboy* and I guarantee this book will teach more about life and business than four years at any Ivy League college.

This is not just another "and then I wrote..." advertising book by another agency chairman. Richie writes about what it takes to lead and motivate people. He writes about dealing with clients, dealing with parents, dealing with marriage, dealing with life.

Want to know the horrors of a Hennessy Cognac shoot with a model who refuses to come out of her trailer because she has to be photographed wearing nothing but a wispy piece of silk and she's cold? What do you do after three hours when she says she won't come out of the trailer unless all the participants in the commercial—client, agency personnel, photographer—strip down naked, too?

Wondering what it's like to direct Andy Warhol in a commercial for a client who had never heard of Andy Warhol?

What happens when Richie tries to talk Miss America Phyllis George into starting a commercial with the words, "I'm here to show America something they've never seen before—my breasts"?

Then read on....

*   *   *   *

It wasn't all just fun and games, though. There was great work for Kenneth Cole, Snapple, Target, Hennessy, and so many others. Some great products succeeded because Richie is so much more than just an advertising writer.

He has the eye of an art director, the ear of a musician, an uncanny fashion sense, and no one in the history of the advertising business has ever had a keener awareness of pop culture. All this from a sweet Jewish prince from Long Island. Go figure.

If my advertising generation owned the 1960s and 1970s and early 1980s, Richie Kirshenbaum owns the late 80s, the 90s, right on to tomorrow.

Imagine *Mad Men* with computers and the Internet.

OK, Richie is no Don Draper in looks, but he's a helluva lot better creative guy.

*　　*　　*　　*

When I finished *Madboy* I thought of Murray.

Murray was a grizzled old art director who got into the advertising business pre-*Mad Men* in the 1940s.

He was a "good old days" guy.

Here we were in 1961, a creative department filled with young kids a generation removed from the original Mad Men, enjoying our role in the new advertising creative revolution.

And Murray would shout, "You guys missed the good old days!"

I guess doing ads with doctors selling Camel cigarettes must have been loads of fun for Murray.

It's clear that Richie had his own "good old days" to write about.

But I don't want to be like Murray.

OK, Richie, I admit it. Your "good old days" sound like a lot more fun and make for better reading than my "good old days."

PROLOGUE

ONE OF THE BEST THINGS about being in the ad business is no two days are alike. That's because no two clients are the same, nor are the problems and the solutions. Which means that you can always wake up and expect the unexpected and, as I like to say, get to be a "jack of all trades, master of *some*." That said, there is the unexpected and the *unbelievable*. And there have been a number of days since founding our advertising agency, Kirshenbaum Bond + Partners (kbp), twenty-four years ago that I can honestly say have fallen into the latter category.

I mean, how many people can say that they've gone to the office and have had Paris Hilton as their secretary (during *The Simple Life*) and had to ask Nicole Richie to make room at the Xerox machine when she was xeroxing her brassiere? Who else can say they appeared on the cover of *Wired* magazine with not only the legendary George Lois but the Pillsbury Doughboy? Or that they were an extra in a Joan Jett video that is now a VH1 Classic? (I am dating myself.) Or opened an office in Ed McMahon's LA house?

When I first entered the ad business in my early twenties, there were pretty much two kinds of agencies: boutique print agencies and those that focused mostly on TV commercials for larger clients (like car companies). There was little thought of bridging them. Until I, at twenty-six, and Jon Bond, at twenty-nine, started kbp. We didn't set out to build that bridge, much less a new concept of advertising. It never occurred to us that there were rules or protocols to follow. We just operated on instinct and our gut.

Perhaps, in retrospect, doing the unconventional, the unexpected, was actually the impetus that led to the unbelievable. After all, in the early days of its inception, kbp became known for breakthrough advertising because it led by inventing and surprising the industry with not only one of the first integrated structures (offering design, public relations, direct mail, interactive services, etc.), but it offered even more. It was one of the first agencies to create under-the-radar and 360-degree marketing solutions (we even wrote a book about this, which is still used as a blueprint for marketing in many universities). We were the first agency to unexpectedly invent street-stenciling, the first agency to invent advertising on fruit, the first agency to invent the pop-up retail store, and one of the first to create brand content—an actual TV show *for* felines (i.e., cats), which provided entertainment for them. It can be argued that we created or at the very least influenced reality TV by having brands we represented—not just products but the real people behind them—filmed and marketed in real time. All this, unusual and unexpected.

Yes, unexpected might have been lecturing at the Harvard Business School (I could never have gotten in there). But unbelievable is going to Sony headquarters and eating popcorn while they are screening Morgan Spurlock's new movie (out in April 2011), which I am actually in. I was watching myself as *myself* on the big screen. Unexpected is growing up to shoot campaigns with supermodels, movie stars, icons like Robert Kennedy Jr. and Muhammad Ali. Unbelievable was being a model myself (for Paul Stuart). Unexpected is being the precursor to advertising and branding via social media—YouTube, Facebook, Twitter—by coproducing creative work that engaged consumers in real dialogue, in real time. Unbelievable is founding a Jamaican rum with Chris Blackwell, founder of Island Records, and having a celebration launch with the prime minister. I've helped cofound two digital and direct-mail marketing companies in this arena, producing huge results.

After all these years, still not knowing what the day or the phone will bring, I have only started to fully embrace the unbelievable or the unexpected and even the ridiculous (try being one of *Us Weekly's* Fashion Police). No one told me that when I started out in the ad biz my job would encompass not just being a copywriter, but part actor, orator, art director, private equity guy, creative director, human resources director, model (literally), TV producer, and reality TV personality with my own show, interviewing creatives at lunch—who had any other time? I didn't realize that there were *that* many facets or expectations to being a successful ad Mad Man.

The company my partner and I founded twenty-four years ago is now part of a public company whose other units are tangential to ours, with more than five hundred employees (we started with two), close to a billion dollars in billing, with seven businesses and offices in three countries. I still marvel at the unexpected. As I write this, I am staring out at Central Park from my new Fifth Avenue duplex. (Ridiculous? You bet.) I look toward the boat pond and remember something else unforgettable and unbelievable—not that long ago I was crashing on my sister's sofa and answering phones working for *free* as a receptionist to get experience at an ad agency. I was brown-bagging lunch in the park, looking at the buildings on Fifth Avenue—including the one I now live in—with awe.

A bit unbelievable? Wait 'til I tell you the rest. . . .

THE COMPETITIVE LANDSCAPE

CHAPTER ONE
MY LONG G'ISLAND ACCENT

MINE IS NOT EXACTLY A rags-to-riches story, but more like a *rag-trade-to-riches* story.

I'm not going to lie and tell you I walked three miles to school or didn't have enough to eat. In fact, memories of my family are all about eating Long Island Jewish style, which meant you had Chinese food at China Jade in Hewlett every Sunday night, and relatives plied you with every conceivable calorie while they pinched your cheeks and told you that you were too thin. And if anyone knows anyone who lives in or around the Five Towns, they will wax poetic about the seven-layer chocolate cake from Wall's Bake Shop, the Hawaiian chicken from Woodro Kosher Deli, the summer snack bar (a scoop of tuna with lemon and a Coke) at the Westbury Beach Club in Atlantic Beach, and all the buffets causing groans at bar mitzvahs, weddings, and sweet sixteens. After all, what's an affair without a good pig in a blanket and a mini eggroll? The food was really a subtext for a personality and style—a sense of sixties' and seventies' affluence and opulence, which was culturally distinct and imbued with flavor and humor. It bridged the gap between the *Goodbye, Columbus* years and the introduction of nouvelle cuisine (i.e., stuffed derma versus the tuna roll) where people ate with abandon, and if someone mentioned anorexia nervosa, they most likely thought it was an opera.

These days, whether someone's living in a penthouse on Park Avenue or the Grand Manor in Greenwich, I can always spot a refugee from the Five Towns (pronounced "foive" towns). The accent, however subtle and redesigned it may be, is a dead giveaway. Every once in a while, I'll be talking to people with airs, and it suddenly slips out. They'll say "like" too much or ask for a glass of "wattah" or they'll carry over the hard "g" when they say "Long G'Island." As in, "Dahling, we winter in Saint Moritz and summer in Southampton. I just adore Long G'Island." (Which, by the way, is still a better pronunciation than Long Goyland.) However, one of the first great lessons I ever learned about being creative is that if you don't embrace who you are and bring your own accent or flavor to your work, you can never truly be creative, authentic, or original. And that's one of the things that I love about my accent. I own it.

The Kirshenbaum family was somewhat of a mix of intelligentsia and high and low oddballs. (My father and his brother actually grew up spelling the last name differently. They have the "c" in Kirsch and we don't. And no one thought this was odd.) It's really no coincidence I went into the ad business. Now that I think of it, you would have, too, particularly if you had a grandfather like mine. Grandpa Harry looms large in my childhood memories because he was indeed *very* large. A very large man with very large opinions. The New York City policeman loved his family and friends foremost, but his brands were not so much a distant second.

BRANDPA

My entire childhood was a dictated list of my grandfather's brand preferences that are permanently etched in my mind. His brands were not only a code of how to enjoy life but how to actually live life, and dissension was not discussed or tolerated. You were either in Brandpa's world, or you weren't. And no one wanted to be banished to brand Siberia. It went something like this: A real man always had an Anheuser-Busch beer waiting in the fridge with a tall glass frosting in the freezer. Van Heusen made the best shirts, lest there be a crease, and you always made a Windsor knot with a Countess Mara tie. Plaid and seersucker were "for suckers," or for men who weren't "dag," or couldn't flaunt it like Frank, Sammy, and Dean—his heroes. Boxers *only*—never would briefs have been considered, and the Izod alligator was a good friend. A real man only smoked unfiltered Camels or Marlboros, wore English Leather, and shaved with a Schick razor. Cadillacs were the "ne plus ultra." A Buick was a good second choice with a Chevy coming in third for affordability. For a man who had something like twenty-eight cars in twenty-three years, I never heard the words Lincoln, Dodge, and Ford uttered. They only existed for "the others," whoever "they" were.

Brandpa in his prime

Brandpa spoke like a character out of *Guys and Dolls,* with a burning cigarette dangling permanently from his lip. He called women dames. He totally bought into stereotypes, which affected his *brand*scape. "Eyetalians made the best semolina bread." You were allowed to drink a German beer like a Becks (because we won the war and his brother Bucky liberated a camp). The Pollacks (pronounced po-lax) knew mustard (Kosciusko the grainy best). Those damn French were "good for nuttin'" because he didn't drink wine ("wine is for pussies"). Entenmann's made the best coffee crumb cake. You only used half and half in your coffee because the best part of waking up was Folgers in your cup or Maxwell House. And if we didn't have Temp Tee whipped cream cheese in the fridge for his his bagels with lox, sliced, with red onion and tomato (a good kike meal), you might as well have declared yourself a commie.

Each room at Brandpa's house had to have at least three to five Sony Trinitrons ("the best color picture") all going at the same time, like an electronics store. Lawrence Welk was a "real gentleman," and *The Jackie Gleason Show* was "filmed right over there on the Causeway!" He would always elbow me when the June Taylor Dancers came on. How sweet it is! Bugs Bunny was funny; you could take anything else. And Miami Beach, where he retired when he was fifty, was the land of Milk of Magnesia, honey, and coconut patties. When he was ninety, he took me aside and gave me his lifelong secret: "Every night take a shot of Johnnie Walker. It's good for you *down there*." He kept a bottle in the bottom of his closet for a handy swig. He looked me coldly in the eye with this fact.

During school holidays, my parents would ship me and my sister, Susan, off to Florida on Delta—the only good airline—because of the orange juice and the fluffy egg-and-cheese omelet breakfast. Once settled in the sunshine state, Brandpa would sit across from me during breakfast in his white-ribbed Hanes wife beater and stubble (like the Jewish Marlon Brando) with a belt ominously on his lap so I would be encouraged to finish my Quaker Oats oatmeal ("it'll put hair on your chest") and down his elixir of life, Tropicana orange juice, perhaps the greatest brand in Brandpa's brand cavalcade. If you didn't start the day with Tropicana, you might as well not get out of bed. My grandmother Elsie and her sisters Lily, Celie, and perhaps cousin Honey would all line themselves up on their identical lounge chairs with their coiffed bouffant hairdos (clouds of Aqua Net or Adorn spray kept them in place) at the Raleigh Pool (voted "most beautiful pool in Florida") and slather me in either Johnson's baby oil and iodine for color or Sea & Ski for protection ("or you'll turn into a lobster").

Does it get any more '60s Miami? Honey, Celia, Lily, and Grandma Elsie

I was always unsure about why Brandpa was so fastidious about his brands until he told me that at age seven he was put to work by his father, Big Grandpa, shoveling coal into the 180-degree furnace of a tenement building on the Lower East Side. Big Grandpa was the building super and, to hear Grandpa tell it, he slept next to the boiler and lived on onion sandwiches on hard black bread. (I loved my Quaker Oats oatmeal and my Tropicana even more after visualizing the image.)

Grandpa's black-and-white attitudes about brands and people sometimes served as cautionary tales. There were a lot of "don'ts." Once when I was seven years old, Brandpa took me to the Boom Boom Room at the Fontainebleau (his cultural equivalent of visiting the Metropolitan Museum of Art). I was ordered to "steer clear of that little old Jewish man" dressed exactly like Brandpa (i.e., white shoes, white belt, and light blue poly Izod button-down acrylic sweater, walking a dog outside the hotel).

"That's Meyer Lansky," my grandfather mentioned, as if at seven, I would know who Meyer Lansky was. "Grandpa," I asked looking up at the looming figure. "Why should I steer clear of him?"

"You'll understand when you're older." He shook the ashes from his Marlboro, his four-carat sapphire-and-diamond pinkie ring glittering in the dusk. "On the other hand," Brandpa said, "he can't be half bad if he's driving a Caddy!"

*   *   *   *

For Brandpa, the sun rose and set on his wife, my grandmother Elsie, who matched Grandpa's brawn with her womanly graces and because her pointy-toed, silk *peau de soie* shoes matched her oversize handbag (very "the Queen Mother"). Not to mention she had "the coin" and provided for all Brandpa's brand needs beyond what his pensions from being a NYC police officer and working for New York Life covered. He had the brawn and Grandma had the "class and the dough." He once gambled away a brownstone of hers for a dollar! Gramps may have stocked up on Camels, but Grandma only smoked Larks. This took on significance. On their fiftieth wedding anniversary, when we asked Brandpa what his golden anniversary gift to Grandma was, he promptly answered "a case of Larks," with Grandma proudly beaming in the background. They were out of Central Casting for the Jewish version of *A Streetcar Named Desire*. He was not exactly PC and was a confident equal opportunity hater. She was sociable and loved everyone.

Grandma Elsie (when I was an adult, someone told me her real name was Agnes—go figure) grew up on the right side of the tracks. Her father owned a very successful button company called Acme Buttons Company at the turn of the century on Lower Broadway. His office was not so far from my own future office, in the Flatiron Building. He was considered creative by producing not only bone but decorative glass and enamel buttons. The one picture of him eerily looks like me with his blond hair. (His Victorian wife and twelve children do not equate.) When he died, Grandma and Aunt Lily opened their own lingerie store with some of their inheritance, called The Lillian Shop. It was next to the moving pictures and sold silk stockings to women even though there were not even sidewalks yet to walk on.

Grandma Elsie and her sister Lily in front of their store

My aunt Lily and uncle Ira lived below my grandparents (like on *I Love Lucy*, and to tell you the truth they looked exactly like Fred and Ethel Mertz, except they didn't have a vaudeville act). When I discovered that my grandfather had actually dated Lily first, it was something of a shock. The only reason I could get about why he left her for my grandmother had something vaguely to do with her having "problems *down there*," but more importantly because he was dismayed that she didn't buy Bumblebee white tuna in oil. (Hence trading her in for my grandmother avoided a historic mismatch.)

To hear Brandpa tell it, he fell in love with Grandma at first sight after seeing her dance the Charleston in a black silk dress (and after dumping poor Aunt Lily). Since he was considered matinee-idol good-looking, but lower class, Grandma did what any self-respecting flapper of that era did who most likely wanted some action. She eloped with him. They got married in the rabbi's study (when she needed a veil, Grandpa characteristically yanked the curtains off the wall in a fit of passion, to the rabbi's chagrin), and then they both went back to living in their parents' houses until someone's parent changed their mind or died.

Once married, they were forced to be separated for vast amounts of time. Since Grandpa had the night shift for years, Grandma never went out socially with him and even took her own vacations. She was more independent than many women of her era and would crank up their Model T and take my mother and my aunt Jackie to Florida in the 1930s before there was even a highway system. My other aunt Lily (I had two) flew in her own plane, or so I'm told, to meet them and Grandma, and she and all her sisters went to the beach, smoked, and went to the beauty parlor. Each wore Pucci-style flowered housedresses and identical bouffant hairdos with little spit curls, except for my aunt Celie, who reminded me of Mae West with her platinum waves. She was a widow whose husband had been mistakenly killed by the coppers in what always felt like a film noir moment, when relatives tried to brush it under the carpet in our presence.

All in all, I never ever heard Grandma say a word against Brandpa. I'm not sure how she handled him. For their entire marriage, he was constantly fixing up an apartment or house and then selling it at a loss and would move the entire family on a whim or would come home with a new car or TV set (the way someone would buy a new pair of trousers). The only time I ever saw Grandma upset was when she and Grandpa went to see the movie *Midnight Cowboy*. She came home, took a tranquilizer, smoked a Lark, and went to bed on her Sealy Posturepedic (the only mattress worth sleeping on). She obviously could deal with Brandpa, but a male prostitute and Dustin Hoffman—that wasn't something she was prepared for.

I remember my grandmother always telling me that I was the apple of her eye. I loved her laugh and hearing her chat on the phone (which was always attached to her ear). She also had her telephone therapy sessions in the kitchen with her psychiatrist, Dr. Rath, who I called The Gripes of Wrath. When I decided to become engaged to my wife, Dana, I called her up on the phone for advice and said, "Grandma, how do you *know*?" I heard her take a drag on her Lark and say, "Darling, you never *know*, but better to be married three or four times than never at all. So why not give it a *whirl*!" Unlike many couples today who call it quits, I still remember their fiftieth wedding anniversary at the Rascal House. Brandpa was upset because we were staying so far *away* (the Doral! Ten blocks from where they lived).

Brandpa may have looked like Marlon Brando, but I was also the only male child in a family of women who had imposing busts and more imposing personalities. So gender stereotypes had little effect on me. I always got along well with women, and this would greatly impact my career. But before I get there, I need to tell you about my sister, and most of all, about my parents.

*   *   *   *

In traditional Jewish households, the mother has special status and the girls, *not the boys,* often tend to get things first (especially if they are older). Given that I grew up with a sister, four girl first cousins, a myriad of female second cousins, and Grandma's "sister/aunt posse," I'm well trained. My sister, Susan, has an Auntie Mame quality about her: vivacious and fun. I adore her, even though she had a competitive advantage growing up.

When I was in college, my parents told me (and my sister) that I was going to get a Volkswagen Rabbit (again, dating myself) that they had used as a station car to take to school. The whole summer, I cleaned, waxed, and polished that car. Susan, who is two and a half years older than me, was leaving for college the day before I was and was catching a ride with one of her friends. Or so I thought. The next day, I couldn't believe my eyes as I saw Susan make a mad dash into the VW and quickly pull out of the driveway, waving and crying, saying "I feel so bad" as she put her foot on the gas and *gunned it*! I still see myself running down the street after her and the car—which got so many parking tickets, it was impounded a few months later in Ohio.

When Susan graduated college, she tried her hand at many things— teaching, real estate—and I was conflicted when she decided to go into the advertising headhunting business. She started as a headhunter working for and becoming a partner with my original headhunter firm where Jill Weingarten and Lori Greenberg worked. At first, I felt she was taking my Volkswagen again, and we agreed not to work together. Today Greenberg Kirshenbaum (a nice *Gentile* firm) is one of the top three well-regarded creative headhunting firms in the business, and I regularly go to Susan for candidates and advice. Her divining rod for talent is by far the best in the biz. But speaking of Gentiles, I can't tell you how many times I've heard non-Jewish women tell me they want me to find them a Jewish husband. At my friend Randy's recent wedding, the rabbi said (to laughs) before he was to break the glass under the chuppah that this is the last time Randy would ever put his foot down. Not so far from the truth.

My mother, Marilyn, had a biting wit and wore the pantsuits in the family. Literally. She always reminded people of the title character of the TV show *Maude*, in her pantsuits and scarves. At my grandparents' fiftieth, I remember that she had a hard time getting into her plaid Texan pantsuit with its requisite seventies' silk blouse and bow. She went into a rage because the zipper didn't work, but I knew she was under *brand pressure* every time she visited Brandpa. Marilyn was also very strong-willed herself, however. She was not one to suffer fools lightly, and she had a sophisticated intelligence. She actually went back to graduate school at a Catholic college, Molloy, in Rockville Centre because she related so strongly to the nuns' sense of discipline. She was a bit out of place in a community populated by "the housewives of Long Island," I think. She was more bookish and eschewed makeup and jewelry. She venerated literature. My father tells my favorite story about her: My mother had her first office job in the 1940s in the city. When her flamboyant boss didn't want her to hear something private, he conversed with his partner in French—until one day, when he was talking about my mother, she answered him back in French. They immediately became fast friends.

Marilyn (a.k.a. Maude) in the 1950s

My father, Stanley Ira, ran a textile company with my uncle called Windjammer Knits. He was both very silly and full of integrity. Stanley Ira was always was a bit of an iconoclast and way ahead of his time. He stood on his head in a yoga pose and juiced carrots from a Braun juicer. He did yoga before everyone else. Imagine growing up in a house where your father was always standing on his head or doing the "sun and moon." The Braun juicer was always going at full speed on liquefy, and I was forced to drink copious amounts of carrot juice and eat Tiger's Milk bars from the natural food store in Hewlett. Once he wore a paste-on earring at a Passover seder and told everyone he thought the government should legalize marijuana, to my uncle's intense chagrin. That is my father to the hilt.

ALTERNA-DAD

I've often thought of Stanley Ira as "Alterna-Dad." In the late sixties, people were having Mad Men martinis for cocktail hour; Stan the Man was drinking his carrot juice. He drove a foreign car instead of an American one (a 1961 Volvo that looked like an armadillo). Other fathers had *Sports Illustrated* delivered; he had French *Elle*! Other fathers spent the day in front of the box watching the game or coaching their sons' Little League games. I was in Greenwich Village bookstores and eating stuffed grape leaves from the now defunct but wonderful Delphi restaurant in Tribeca, while Dad was reading aloud passages from *The Good Earth.*

Stanley Ira always did things first. He was first to shop and cook (a woman's job) and always said the best chefs in Europe were men. That said, my most intense gestational memory of my father taking me to my favorite restaurant, R. Gross, in the Garment Center. In those days, it was a dairy restaurant on Broadway, and all the moguls came there to eat there. The stretch limos would drop off Sol or Irving; either thin, tan, weathered men in big black-framed glasses (à la Lew Wasserman) or big, rotund fellows who wheezed their way through the revolving door. They came for the

Alterna-Dad, Stanley Ira K.

world's best cheese and kasha blintzes and potato pancakes. These pancakes—the size of saucers, fried to a golden brown and served with snowdrifts of sour cream and tart applesauce—were slammed down in front of you by the rudest, but greatest, waitstaff this side of Riga.

Stanley Ira was one of the first people I knew who collected photography and thought it was "art." I witnessed firsthand how conventional people at the time could not understand how a "reproduced" photo could be in the same league as a painting or sculpture, and he took major shit for it. My father never wavered on his opinion, though. He took us to the Whitney and galleries in New York to look at Man Ray and Jacques-Henri Lartigue. He loved George Tice and Edward Weston before they ever had major museum shows. While we spent a great deal of time at the Met and the Museum of Modern Art, my father also loved American painting, and I remember the skillful colors of the Milton Avery show. I became a member of the photography committee at the Whitney in my thirties because I understand and appreciate my father's aesthetics. And I have brought the understanding of the impact photography can make into my work, from the very beginning.

Overall, Alterna-Dad's perceptions and way of thinking have always had a huge effect on me. Once when I was sixteen and Brandpa was reviewing my scrawny frame in a bathing suit, he shook his head wistfully. "Well, ya didn't get my body, but at least ya got your fadder's brains!" I wasn't sure what I was supposed to make of that but Stanley Ira's different way of thinking paved the way for some of my seemingly effortless, but often remarked "Bold Moves." Indeed, I employ Alterna-Dad's way of thinking to most business-related issues today. It's not challenging the status quo for the sake of challenging—it's asking why or why not when most people are just accepting of everything the way that it is. Kbp was founded on such thinking, which has manifested itself in such creative ways. Why do we need to actually show a product in an ad (we didn't in our first ad, for Kenneth Cole)? Why is advertising limited to the written page (we put ads on fruit for Snapple)? Why don't advertising agencies advertise (more on this and all of the above later . . .)? Why, why, why?

None of this is to say that that my father wasn't a conventional dad, too. He yearned for conventional things as well, but he was and is an unconventional thinker relative to his peer group and generation. "A company job? Why would anyone want to work for (some putz) when you could be your own boss?" said Stanley Ira. Alterna-Dad knew that as conventionally comfortable as it would have felt for *me* to have gone into textiles, it would have been a mistake. The Garment Center was in its last glory days, and he predicted that the great textile mills of the South would close and all the production would eventually move off-shore to Asia. He was right and did nothing to encourage me to go into the rag trade. Perhaps it would have been easier, but less satisfying, if I had a family real estate business to go into, or if Daddy or Grandpa were the "salami kings of the Northeast." But although I had all the trimmings and Stan could claim inventing knit Ultrasuede, a life working at the family factory and a membership to Seawane (the country club I affectionately dubbed *seawhine*) was not in the cards for yours truly. What's more, the typical thought of going to typical med school didn't sound quite appealing, either. This said, I was distantly related to a very successful dermatologist who built one of the first modern mansions in Hewlett Harbor. My mother affectionately dubbed it the "pimple palace." I could neither boast an interest in pustules or the legal system or manipulating numbers, therefore abrogating the Jewish trinity: doctor, lawyer, and accountant.

But, of course, before career directions came into any true focus there would be college, and before college there were all sorts of childhood regimens—and perks. And they, too, made their mark on my way of navigating the world. For some reason, my parents saw my lack of interest in the mundane as a celebrated elitist trait (yah) and rewarded me by sending me on an eight-week bus tour of Europe, with forty other spoiled and indulged sixteen- and seventeen-year-olds. I, of course, chose the five-star hotel tour, which they agreed to do because in my house five stars would mean better accommodations (read: food). So I waltzed over the continent staying in villa-style rooms at swish places like the Marbella Club, and buying suede and leather products in Florence and sandals in Capri. The lack of interest among the other kids (mostly from Beverly Hills, Miami, and Long Island) to see or appreciate any of the major cultural sites of Europe was highlighted by one girl (I dated her) who wouldn't get off the bus to see the Eiffel Tower. She would only disembark for food or a Louis Vuitton store within walking distance.

When I returned, it was time (well past time) for me to start getting serious about applying to colleges and think about potential career choices. So what does the supremely sensitive, creatively oriented, directionless child do? Well, if he's living off the LIE, the obvious thing to do was to have his parents pay to go to a college/career counselor who would supposedly match potential colleges with potential careers. Kind of like a pay-for-play crystal ball.

After my parents sent in the check, the day of the highly anticipated visit arrived. It started with a test that felt like the SAT I had recently taken for college, where I filled in boxes with a lead pencil. But these questions were not SAT ones. "Do you prefer to make a macramé plant holder or chop wood?" was one of them.

A woman with a lacquered beehive and one of those 1970s half-eaten ceramic apples hanging from a rawhide string evaluated my answers and interests. Afterward, my mother and I were summoned into her small gray cubicle, where we waited with bated breath to hear what career path I should take after graduating from the appropriate college. The evaluator reviewed my test scores with a sour look. "Well, given you have no interest in typical things *other* young men seem to like—like sports, medicine, mathematics, or becoming a judge—it appears to me that . . ."

"Yes." We leaned forward as if listening to the oracle from Delphi.

"You might want to . . . well, there's an art school in Sarasota—no, I mean the other coast of Florida—that was endowed by the Ringling family . . . for the arts." She coughed.

"The Ringling Brothers?! I paid for this exam, and you're suggesting my son run away and join the circus?" My mother sat, protectively clutching her Pierre Deux quilted bag to her chest as if it was a bulletproof vest. She had just been shot.

"It's very prestigious in some circles. Look, it's not like this one's going to go to Carnegie Mellon." She munched on a dry piece of celery. Deflated, we thanked her. And I stood thinking that while a flaming hoop and a trapeze seemed novel, it really didn't cut it for me. "What, you don't like the performing arts?" she asked, registering the look on my face as she looked up from her soggy tuna sandwich. "Well, hon, if all else fails you can always go into advertising."

She laughed.

CHAPTER TWO
BOY FRIDAY BECOMES ADBOY

SILENCE CAN BE DEAFENING. ESPECIALLY when your mother is on the other end of the phone.

"You're making how much?" Her voice flat-lined.

"Well, that's just it. I did get the job . . . the only thing is, it's not really a job yet, more like a job/internship/competition."

"Are you getting paid or not?"

"Well, it's for free until she decides to hire me or the other guy, Mom."

If a tree falls in the forest and no one hears it, did it fall? And if your mother doesn't answer you, was she angry or on the other end of the phone at all? Finally, I heard breathing. "Perhaps the circus option would have been more profitable, but if this makes you happy. . . ." It is a given that my debut into the workforce was neither prestigious nor profitable. Yet I was so excited, I felt like I was walking on air. "Walking on air," you might ask, "to be working for free?" Working as a boy Friday, and in competition for a job that would pay the princely sum of nine thousand dollars per annum, should I be lucky enough to get it.

My mother's stony silence and chilly reception to my news were not only about the pay. Marilyn (a.k.a. Maude) thought a college degree at a "private university not a state school, mind you" meant something. What it didn't mean was "working for free, and on the phones." I also had to readjust my thinking. After our wonderful session with the college and career counselor, I had achieved a small triumph by gaining admission to the prestigious S. I. Newhouse School of Public Communications at Syracuse University, and so visions of training programs at firms like

Ogilvy & Mather and requisite starting salaries danced in my head. But none had materialized. In all honesty, I'd gamed the system a bit to get in. If my memory serves me correctly, first I entered the school of retailing and then I declared Newhouse my dual major, since I wasn't able to gain admission first off to the prestigious communications school. As the old saying goes, "If they don't let you in through the door, go in through the window." Clearly, retailing was better than the big top, but it was largely a creation populated by Long Island and New Jersey princesses who had money but needed career direction. As in "OK, Stacey or Mindy, you're not too bright, the only thing you're interested in is shopping and guys, sooooo the school of retailing is just for you!" I was in one class where the professor actually held up a garment and said, "This . . . is a mini-skirt!" to an enthralled group of girls who oohed and aahed and took copious notes, as if recording a lecture on Darwin.

I'd also joined the fraternity ZBT (called Zionist Bankers Trust behind our backs by the other fraternities). It was a clearinghouse for the rich and spoiled sons of the South Shore and North Shore, with some Star Island, Miami, thrown in for good measure. Nearly everyone had a family business to go into. The pecking order was determined by the size of your allowance and what kind of car your drove. Like the luxury car dealership on Northern Boulevard in Great Neck, the ZBT parking lot was overflowing with BMWs and Mazda RX-7s and 280Zs, either in black or red (it was the eighties after all). I barely gained admission with my black Subaru, so I was low on the pecking order. I was also considered somewhat of an oddball because I was in Newhouse, wrote for the school paper ("he must be really smart"), and was considering a career in something creative (hence undecipherable) that was *not* going to be the rag trade or real estate.

After graduation, I was sitting in the land of unemployment (the deck in my backyard) when I defined my creative career. My father brought out a glass of freshly squeezed carrot juice and a copy of the *Wall Street Journal*. I promptly poured the carrot juice into the flowerbeds behind me, but I quickly devoured the front-page article about a new advertising agency and its founder, Lois Korey. There was one of those wonderful line drawings, which endeared me to her immediately. The piece also included a profile of her early years writing for the show of shows—Ernie Kovacs—with Woody Allen as her writing partner.

Mentioning Woody Allen to anyone on Long Island is akin to the faithful mentioning the Pope. So that tasty tidbit from Lois's résumé got me thinking. Within fifteen minutes, I had written a comedic monologue about what it was like to be unemployed, and it had two endings in which Lois would control my fate. Version One ended with her not hiring me, and I led a life in leather underwear. In Version Two, she did hire me and I lived a lifetime in bliss. "You can't send a woman like that something like this!" my mother intoned, sounding and looking quite like Maude in her pantsuit and scarf as she walked into the kitchen with dramatic flair. I took that as a good sign and promptly walked my monologue to the corner mailbox, sending it on its merry way.

Now here's the rub. Twenty-five years later, I still cannot comprehend nor understand nor believe that the letter was actually mailed and delivered in twenty-four hours. But I swear (sweaaar!—and that's with a full Long G'Island accent). I sweaaar, it got there overnight. The very next day, I was sitting on the deck in the same laconic position, with my trusty blue reflector and baby oil for a good summer burn (sweaaar), dumping another glass of carrot juice into the flowerbeds, when Marilyn (a.k.a. Maude) opened up the screen door and said, "She's on the phone."

"Who's she?" I said, thinking it was my childhood stalker, Nora Lapidus, whose brothers always threatened to beat me up unless I danced with her to "Stairway to Heaven" at Camp Naticook's prom every summer. I shrugged.

"It's not Nooora!" my mother intoned, having screened a million phone calls from the infatuated. "It's Lois Korey. She wants to talk to you *now*."

I really do not know what I was thinking when I chose my one gray interview suit, gray leather disco pumps, and a fake but flashy Canal Street Patek Philippe watch set off against my feathered Barry Gibb mop. All topped off with my very Nancy-looking black portfolio case with its weak supply of handwritten and drawn ads. Now there is a great divide between those of us who entered the workforce BC and those of us who came later. That's Before Computers, guys. And while I'm still considered relatively young in the ad biz in my forties, I had a hand-drawn portfolio back then. Compared to the computer-generated realism of today's student books, I might as well have been wearing a stovepipe hat and talking about the Battle at Gettysburg. That said, I thought I was the bomb.

Anyway, Lois Korey and her partner, Allen Kay, had gone out on their own after working for larger agencies, and they'd hung out their shingle in an imposing townhouse on Seventy-fifth Street between Fifth and Madison avenues. It certainly wasn't a conventional place to start a business, but true to Lois's flair and sense of style, it was luxurious and made an immediate impression. I fell in love with Lois the moment her secretary ushered me into her office, which was a grand beaux-arts living room with two partners' desks facing each other under the window.

"So you're the one that wrote the letter?" she said dryly. "Allen, he's the boy who wrote the letter. Funny." Lois rose from her desk. She was an attractive, well-put-together woman with blonde, coiffed hair, and a warm, pretty smile. Bronx-bred, she was a successful, worldly woman and had perfected that expensive Manhattan uptown style (you know; sufficiently understated in an overstated kind of way). From her collapsible ivory bifocals to her Chanel cap-toe shoes, she smelled like a million, and it was Fracas all the way. She linked my arm and walked me through the office. "So how would you like to learn how to write copy?"

"I'd love to," I gushed.

"Well, since we've just started out, we cannot afford to pay you. But if you would like to work for me for the summer, I will teach you, and at the end of the summer I'll decide."

"Decide what?"

"Decide who gets the job. We already have one other intern for the summer," she said as she led me down the stairs to meet my competition. My bubble burst when I met Jim Grace. I joked, "As in the Grace Building?" He nodded.

Jim was sitting at an upright artist's desk when he looked up at me. His classic blond hair and blue eyes were complemented by his Harvard pedigree. Of course, I thought the fix was in, especially when I found out his great-grandfather had been mayor of New York. But we would become fast friends, and we were supportive of each other instead of competitive. After a polite but forced introduction, Lois escorted me back upstairs to have Allen take a look at my portfolio. I sat there as he flipped quickly through my book and kept uttering, "This has to pass my who-gives-a-shit test. Who gives a shit, who gives a shit . . ." he said, looking at my work with barely a glance at me.

"Allen, don't be mean. He's cute and funny." I sat there watching them as Lois was finishing a letter to a client. "Allen, what's that other word, you know, for native?"

"Indigenous," I offered.

"You're hired." She smiled. "For the summer."

As I look back, the summer had a golden patina. I crashed at my sister's apartment and slept on the pull-out gray-flannel deco sofa she'd gotten at the Bloomingdale's clearance center.

There's something about starting at the very bottom that I highly recommend to the young and entitled. You get to feel good about your abilities and the payoff from doing motivated work, not from what you have, where you live, or what your last name is. I was also in the first generation of men to work for the first generation of female executives. When I first started on the phones, I felt a bit weird. But within a day or two, I was happily pouring coffee for clients, bringing in Lois's dry-cleaning, rolling rugs, and relishing in the joy of writing copy and having Lois critique it. Luckily for me, one of my first assignments was a print campaign for El Al Airlines (not a big stretch for me). Lois loved my headline, "Why is this flight different than all other flights?" (For the Gentiles in the room, the line "why is this night different than all other nights" is a famous Passover seder question.) Lois also had me write copy for radio ads. My radio commercial for the Virgin Airways debut, "Food, wine, and an English virgin for only 169 dollars," was an instant hit, and it ran immediately.

Lois gave generously of her time and explained to me that good copy is not how people write grammatically, but how people speak. And she taught me the importance of bringing my voice and tone into my writing. Lois showed me some of the well-known work she and Allen had created: the famous Xerox campaign that used monks to highlight the benefits of Xerox's new quiet machine, and her hysterical commercial featuring Dr. Joyce Brothers's mother for Goodman's egg noodles. That one brought Lois's own comedic flair to life. And many nights, I would drop off packages at her glamorous apartment on Park Avenue and Eightieth Street. (Years later, in a weird twist, I would rent the apartment a floor below Lois's in the same building while I was renovating my own apartment. Given she had sadly passed on years before, I actually thought she had directed me there.)

Every day was fresh and exciting. Each lunchtime, I would take my brown bag sandwich to the park and sit by the sailboat pond, looking up at the buildings peeking over the trees in the park and asking myself who lived there. The mansions of Hewlett Harbor were still impressive, but there was a whole new level of sophistication and taste here in the city. New York was fabulous, dangerous, and decadent in the early eighties. And while I was working the phones by day, I was meeting up with my college friends by night, getting into the (then) novel nightclubs—Studio 54 and Area. Jim also took me to have lunch in the venerable Fifth Avenue building he grew up in, and the staff welcomed him with, "Master Grace, it's so good to see you." We lunched in the building's private dining room, where we were served sandwiches (with no crust) by white-gloved waiters, all of which reminded me of an Edith Wharton novel. I regaled him with stories about R. Gross and felt sorry for him. Although he had grown up in something like a twenty-seven-room full-floor apartment, the food on Fifth Avenue sucked! I didn't dream that a few years later I would have my own agency, that Jim would become one of my first employees, and that I would be living on Fifth Avenue myself, overlooking the park, and only a block away from where I was answering the phones. "Good morning, Korey Kay and Partners, how can I help you?"

THE STRATEGY

CHAPTER THREE
BIG DREAMS, BIG PERSONALITIES, AND ANDY WARHOL

AT THE END OF THE summer, I got the internship job and spent a glorious year under Lois's tutelage. That said, it's not that easy to live in New York City on nine thousand dollars a year, no matter how thrifty you are (and friends, this was still 1983, not 1883). Given the volume of work I was selling, I knew I would always be underpaid and considered "the former receptionist," not a high-powered copywriter. The need to make a switch had become clear. Not to mention, I was tired of sleeping on the pull-out sofa. My sister's apartment abutted the bedroom of the woman who lived next door. Let's just say she "entertained" men. Each night, I fell asleep to some artful screaming and thumping. I decided it was time to get my own place in addition to a new job.

I went to a headhunter, Jill Weingarten. Shortly, she and her blue-eyed colleague Lori Greenberg called me and stated with conviction, "There's this young guy who's going to take over the world. He's currently taking over his father's company, a small but well-regarded agency. You should meet him." I could hear her taking a drag on a cigarette over the phone.

David Deutsch Associates was a small "boutique" agency that specialized in tasteful and elegant print campaigns and radio commercials. Twenty-five years ago, agencies, for the most part, were either large TV agencies, which handled large packaged goods or car accounts, or they were small creative boutique agencies more focused on print campaigns. Donny was on a mission to transform his father's small but well-regarded print agency from a boutique into one of the first independent players.

And it was easy to see, just from meeting him, that he wasn't going to settle for anything less.

Donny Deutsch strolled in with his 'fro, clogs, and gold chain adorning his hairy chest. Forget *The Man in the Gray Flannel Suit*. Donny had balls, and given his skintight jeans, he was happy to show them off to a bevy of willing blondes and brunettes. Within fifteen minutes of looking at my portfolio (and playing a little Jewish geography), Donny offered me a job. Jill later called to confirm the offer: twenty-five thousand dollars a year, and junior copywriter as a title! I literally skipped down the street thinking I was rich, hit the jackpot, and what would I spend all that money on? When the time came for me to tell Lois I was leaving, I sheepishly walked into her office and broke the news. She just looked up at me from her desk as she was applying a fresh coat of coral lipstick. "Well, the mother is always the last to know," she said. As much as I loved Lois and hated to flee the nest, I was in a hurry.

My time at Deutsch really coincided with the last official days of Mad Men. The office was a 1960s chrome-and-marble affair on Third Avenue, and my little office had a wonderful view of the top of the Chrysler Building, which would later be an inspiration for one of my own agency's first ads for the retailer Charivari. The senior executives all wore suits and ties and many had long martini lunches. David Deutsch himself, was a sharp contrast to Donny. They seemed not only unrelated, but from different cultures altogether. (Although I think, as Donny has gotten older, he has started to resemble his father a bit more.) David was tall and slender with gray hair, spectacles, and a pristine bow tie—always the gentleman. I felt very adult as I mixed in a more corporate environment, and the bustle of commuters near Grand Central was a backdrop right out of a Cary Grant film. I was put on the newer accounts with Donny and paired with the vice-chairman of the company, Rocco Campanelli, to work on print accounts like Oneida silverware. Rocco reminded me of a nautical Jim Backus with his sailor's cap, cigar, and glasses. He had the most tasteful design sense and infectious laugh, and he is still a big part of my life. As Lois had been my copywriting mentor, Rocco's elegant and iconic design sensibility was also to have a huge influence on my work.

Rocco was a modern-day artist who understood the idea that less is more, and his print layouts still stand the test of time for their elegance and simplicity.

It was a much simpler time, then, in some ways. No computers, BlackBerries, or cell phones. It's hard to imagine. All layouts were done with Pentel color markers on sheets of tracing paper, which we would put up on a bulletin board with thumbtacks. Because of this, the process was actually more creative as clients and agency creatives had to use their imagination a bit more. And the end result was much more open to interpretation.

As Jill predicted, Donny was indeed going places and was in no mood to sit idle. Pontiac was in the market for a new agency. We immediately pitched to the local Pontiac dealers and got the account, taking David Deutsch Associates from a sleepy print shop to a real TV agency. And one with momentum to boot. (Donny eventually rebranded it as Deutsch and gave it a sleek, new, youthful appearance to mirror his own energy and ideas, propelling it to be one of the great agency success stories.)

I was excited to work for Donny, and on Pontiac, and my ability to write funny radio copy (thanks to Lois) was noticed by the Pontiac client. I started selling and producing work right away. The national theme for the Pontiac dealers was "We build excitement," and Donny had a fresh and interesting campaign idea. It was to ask the question "What was the most exciting thing that ever happened to you?" and then cut to the national "We build excitement" theme with car footage. We worked to break this campaign first with real people on the street, and then with actors. One day, I was sitting in my office, and I thought it could be wonderful to put a celebrity or two into the campaign. Perhaps we should use someone famous and iconic to make it even edgier. No sooner did I start making calls to talent agencies when, as if on cue, I got a call from Paige Powell whom I knew from *Interview* magazine.

"Hi, Richard, word on the street is that you guys are doing great things, and I just want to let you know that Andy Warhol loves the campaign and would like to be in it."

"What?" I couldn't believe my ears. "Andy Warhol would like to be in the Pontiac campaign?"

"Yes," she said. "He likes advertising."

I ran down the hall, told Donny that this was the greatest coup in the world, and called the silver-haired Pontiac client to break the news. "Hi there," I said. "You will never believe this, but Andy Warhol wants to be in our Pontiac campaign."

There was silence on the other end of the phone, finally punctuated by words I thought I'd never hear.

"Who's Andy Warhol?"

"Who is Andy Warhol?" I exclaimed. "Why, he's only the most famous artist of the last half of the twentieth century."

"Never heard of him," he said.

"But it's too good to be true, we have to use him!" I said with youthful enthusiasm.

"Why should I use someone I never heard of?" he said without emotion.

Sometimes in my life, I kick myself for the things I have failed to say in the moment. But this wasn't one of them. "I have an idea. Why don't you go home and ask your wife who Andy Warhol is," I said dramatically. "If she doesn't know, then we don't have to use him."

The next day, I got a call from the client saying Andy Warhol was his wife's favorite artist, and we got the green light. It all happened quickly. The shoot took place in the Factory, in the East Twenties. Andy Warhol looked exactly like, well, Andy Warhol with his spiky white wig. He seemed to have a fairly droll and dry sense of humor. The way it worked was that the director would shoot the cameo of Andy upfront, and once we had the takes we liked, we would edit and cut to the car footage. When it came time to shoot Andy, he stood quietly and without much emotion in front of a large diamond dust canvas. I had prepared some lines for him, one of which answered our tag line query. The director asked Andy, "What was the most exciting thing that ever happened to you?" Andy stared straight at the camera and answered in a high-pitched voice, "I went to the opening of an envelope."

We tried this numerous times, but what had appeared to be a clever line on paper didn't seem to have any sparkle or energy. Finally, exasperated, I asked Andy if he wouldn't mind holding a prop, perhaps his little pug would do the trick. Andy picked up his little dog, and the director asked the question again. Lightning struck. Just as if on cue, the dog yawned, and Andy looked at him with a wide-eyed stare at exactly the right time. Everyone laughed, and we knew we had magic in the can.

When the commercial broke, it caused quite a stir in the press, and at the end of the year *Forbes* magazine nominated it as one of the best auto commercials of 1985. I recall the client bragging, "I'm so glad I thought of using Andy Warhol. One of the best ideas I've ever had." Over the years, people have always asked me how I have dealt with things like this, and all I will say on the subject is, "That's the business we signed up for, making someone else look good." That said, I will now say, "Show

Which one's Andy?

some appreciation, men. The women usually do." Andy was so pleased; he also gave me one of my greatest ad souvenirs, a personally signed copy of *Interview* magazine with Madonna on the cover. It reads, "To Richard from Andy Warhol." So if you ever have to use the loo in my Hamptons house, you will encounter Andy and Madonna over the toilet.

A year went by quickly, and once again I started to get that itch. Working for Donny couldn't have been more fun. I've always considered him to be my big brother in the ad biz. Our working relationship was always punctuated by laughs and felt like an average day in the fraternity. Working for both Lois and Donny were warm, nurturing experiences. Culturally, it felt like family and in the early days Deutsch was still a family business. However, I did know that in the end it would never be *my* family business. I also knew, given my upbringing, that I needed to have a different cultural experience to grow. Despite the access to things my accent gave me, it would do me good to stretch my wings in a totally new way. At Deutsch, I had worked on a mix of big and small accounts from Air Afrique to Saudi Arabian Airlines, hence claiming to possibly be the only person who has worked for an Israeli airline and one featuring a man in an *abaya*. My headhunter, Jill, called me and I called her back from a pay phone for privacy (those were pre-cell phone days).

"Do you know there is an opening at J. Walter Thompson?"

"No."

"Do you know there is an opening in the all-female team?" No, who knew they had one?

"Do you know who the creative director is? The Dragon Lady of Madison Avenue?"

"No."

"Have you ever heard of the chief creative officer?"

"No," I said.

Then she said that while JWT was still considered a hotbed of WASPdom, maybe it was worth a shot. In the eighties, it was still somewhat segregated among certain agencies. Grey, run by Ed Meyer, was of course a Jewish agency with its top management, but it also had a mix of Jews and non-Jews. Young & Rubicam (Y&R), on the other hand, always had a fairly non-Jewish reputation. In fact, many years later, they would ask my business partner and I to consider the possibility of taking over the agency. I called my accountant, David Weiner, and told him about the interest from Y&R and his response was "that's like putting mayonnaise on matzo." While the creative revolution of the 1960s took the ad biz to a more diverse place with the inclusion of Jews (often writers) and Italians (often art directors), the business still had certain fixed reputations, like certain clubs. To this day, we still need to encourage the business to be more inclusive, and I am currently working on a program to help attract more African Americans and Latinos to the business, but more on that later!

"WHY CAN'T WE DO ADS LIKE THIS HERE?"

Before I went for my interview at J. Walter Thompson, Jill sat me down and said point-blank, "Look, JWT has a lot of talented people, but it's still pretty white bread over there. But hey, you've got blond hair and wear Polo, so maybe they'll like you." I, of course, took this comment to the extreme and went to the interview practically wearing an ascot with a mallet. I was going to have an interview with the chief creative director. He was James Patterson.

Before you entered James Patterson's office, you saw that he had stenciled the words *startle me* on the door. He hadn't written *Along Came a Spider* yet, but he was still pretty intimidating, with penetrating eyes and from what I gathered, a droll sense of humor. I didn't know at the time that he would become one of the bestselling authors in the world, but I was in the presence of someone I knew was inspiring. Jim ushered me into his office and indicated I sit on a couch. He briefly looked through my portfolio and talked to me about the available position. It seemed that J. Walter Thompson had an all-female group since the fifties that just handled "women's products," like hair color and douches and the like. Even though it was now the eighties, they had yet to find or hire a male they could all agree on to integrate into that group to handle some of these accounts. Was I interested in working on Reynolds Wrap? Did I think I could do that? Who *me*? Little did Jim know that Grandma Elsie regularly sent her torpedo brassieres up from Florida to New York to get fixed since she and her sisters had closed down their own store a number of years before. I didn't know what kind of fixing they needed, but I was sent to Mary Lerner of Cedarhurst, where I would unfurl them on the counter for repair, throwing them down the way other young guys would bring in their hockey gear.

To think that I broke the gender code at JWT was satisfying, I suppose, but I was perplexed as to why many of the other creative directors seemed to be ex-football players. Perhaps it had something to do with the fact that JWT was the advertising heavyweight with big macho clients like Ford and Kodak. I was playing in the big league now. I had my own office, in which I put a beach lounge chair and a blow-up palm tree for effect. The $47,500-a-year salary finally enabled me to live on my own, and I rented my first apartment at 300 Mercer Street. I was pumped to move into my first bachelor pad, decorating it very "eighties" with black leather and metal shelves from Conran's. When I had my first house-warming party, one of my creative directors took me aside and asked me, "Why do Jews always live in doorman buildings?" I couldn't quite comprehend the question, but might have just replied, "Because we do." And then added, "It's always good to have a first line of defense."

A girl I was friendly with at Syracuse, through the ZBT network, had moved in across the street on Astor Place with her fiancé. I'd always liked Wendy Sachs; while she was small in stature, she had a big, warm person-ality and a hearty laugh. We ran into each other in the street and briefly caught each other up on life post-Syracuse. She said I should meet her fiancé, Jonny, who she said I had lots in common with. He was in the ad business too, also having had a short stint at Korey Kay.

So Jon Bond appeared in my life, reminding me of the Michael J. Fox character in *Family Ties*. In his late twenties, Jon was young, scrappy, and wanted to set the world on fire, like Donny did. His energy was infec-tious. He was currently working as an account executive at an agency called Sacks (no relation to Wendy) & Rosen. I was quite surprised to learn that he had once (when he was about twelve?) started an agency of his own called Grossich & Bond. That sounded very . . . appealing . . . to me and not long after we met, we both decided to freelance together, which many ad people do on the side to earn some extra cash. We wanted to earn some extra money to go to some good restaurants (since we both really liked good food) and we weren't earning big salaries or possessing fat expense accounts yet.

Jon was canvassing accounts for Sacks & Rosen (and would become the best new biz guy in the business). He occasionally came across smaller opportunities for freelance as the accounts he was canvassing weren't always interested in a traditional agency relationship. These were great opportunities for us. We presented ourselves as the classic combination of a creative guy (the hair) and the account guy (the suit). While Jon was also creative and I had a business side to me, we were smart enough to keep this to ourselves. We understood it was almost theatrical, the roles we played. And clients "got it." When they looked at us, they understood the division of labor. We called our little freelance unit Lunch Hour Limited, since it was really limited to the hour we had for lunch and we were doing it to pay for nice places to eat.

Jon and I realized that we worked very well together (*and quickly*) and we soon started landing small assignments for clients wanting an ad or two here or there. Clients like the retailer Beltrami on Fifth Avenue and a restaurant called Hamburger Harry's. One day Jon called me up, quite excited, and said, "I went to meet this young guy named Kenneth Cole, and he had a great office with lots of beautiful girls. He doesn't like ad agencies, but I think you two would get along. Maybe you could persuade him to give us an assignment. I think he's also from Long Island." I don't know why I became interested in meeting with him, but it did sound like he had a great hip, young company. And even if Kenneth Cole didn't like ad agencies, he still needed to do *some* advertising. So I started calling Kenneth's office, trying to get an appointment. And the "Long G'Island" didn't hurt. I just knew if he met with us both we could land this account, or at least get a small gig.

One great thing about having started out as a receptionist is that I understood the mindset of someone answering phones. People (self-important ones, in particular) are incredibly rude and short with receptionists and secretaries, expecting them to know who they (the Important Ones) are. I played the opposite and got Kenneth's assistant laughing at some of my jokes. Soon we had established a rapport, and I said that Kenneth needed to meet me because I was "great!" While Kenneth initially turned us down, his assistant, Courtney, agreed to set up an appointment.

Rule number one in business: Always be nice to the assistant.

Kenneth was exactly as Jon described him; young, handsome, and hip (and hailing from Great Neck), with a bevy of beautiful women. They, in turn, were surrounded by white shoe boxes overflowing with shoes. Kenneth looked at my work and reiterated what Jon had said. "I don't like agencies and I'm not interested." Still, he was running *some* advertising. I pointed to an ad on his desk and asked him if he thought it was great. I think he placated me with, "Well, since you think you're great, if you ever have something great to show me, I'm open to seeing it."

Jon and I had a phone call late that evening to try to crack open the account. What would it take? Earlier that day, I had seen in the paper a story about Imelda Marcos and her controversial shoe collection. We brainstormed together on that idea and created our very first ad together: "Imelda Marcos bought 2,700 pairs of shoes. She could've at least had the courtesy to buy a pair of ours."

> "Imelda Marcos bought 2,700 pairs of shoes.
>
> She could've at least had the courtesy to buy a pair of ours."
>
> —Kenneth Cole

Our first ad for Kenneth

We knew it was timely and clever, and there was something in the current events angle. I had my cousin Vicky, who was an artist, lay out the ad for me in a very simple black-and-white typeface and style. The idea was that Kenneth would sign the ad with his signature. Just a statement in black and white. Occasionally, in the ad business, you know you have a great idea. You can feel it in your belly. And when that happens, you can't wait to present it, sell it, and run it.

The very next day, I called Courtney, promising we had something spectacular (and great) to show her and Kenneth. When we appeared in Kenneth's office, he took one look at the ad and said those magic words, which I always love hearing, "Run it."

The combination of the wit, timing, and current events set a PR wave in motion when the ad first ran in the *New York Times*. Besides hitting a nerve with the public, it was one of the first ads not to show a product, and also to have a negative message sell it (i.e., Imelda *didn't* buy his shoes, as opposed to implying she did). People have commented over the years that they'd never seen an ad or a piece of communication like the early Kenneth Cole ads. The voice was refreshing and honest.

A month later, I was sitting in my office at J. Walter Thompson, and my creative director came in. Even though I had achieved some success by naming a new interactive company, calling it Prodigy, she laid the Imelda ad on my desk, and said, "Why can't we do ads like that here?" I said, "I did that ad. I quit." Jon left his job as well, and we pooled whatever money we had (mine was my bar mitzvah money). The very next day, we started our own agency called Kirshenbaum Bond + Partners. We had our first client, Kenneth Cole. I was twenty-six and Jon twenty-nine. We were so young; we didn't know it was possible that we couldn't do it. And so we did.

THE PITCH

CHAPTER FOUR
OUR FIRST REAL OFFICE, SOLID GOLD

JON AND I STARTED WORKING from the back room of my friend Mitchell Mark's real estate company, First New York Realty. We rented a small room with no air-conditioning for the princely sum of six hundred dollars a month. I'll never forget typing our first ad invoice on a manual typewriter, not quite understanding what I was doing. A month later, a check came back. I was really floored (it was like discovering the charms in Lucky Charms!). After a few months at First New York, mingling with all the real estate brokers, we would often put our own sign over theirs when we had meetings (hence giving a much larger impression). I'll never forget one of our first clients, Marty Tudor, who worked for Dino De Laurentiis, scratching his head at all the brokers and saying, "How long have you been in business?"

Clearly, after we started getting business we needed to find an actual office to hang out our shingle. The space we found and rented at 1133 Broadway (long, long before the area had a hint of chic) was in an old mercantile building, and our office was above an Indian restaurant. I can still smell the wafting curry. When you rent an office and you can't even afford to build walls to create offices, you really have to go out of your way to be creative. Which Mark Zeff did. Mark was in our social circle and an extraordinarily talented young architect and designer from South Africa who would soon become well known. Mark reminded me of a continental Richard Benjamin. He had a keen eye, discerning taste, and was one of the few people his age who could get away with wearing an ascot.

Working around our budget (none), Mark came up with the unique idea to actually create fabric walls (since we couldn't afford the build out!). When I walked him through the raw space and I took him into what eventually would be the conference room, he immediately closed his eyes and waved his hands as if the "design spirit" had entered him. I'll never forget when he said, "We'll just throw up some iron dividers and fabric in the main space and for the conference room, I see gold, gold, gold. We'll spray-paint everything gold for *success*." I immediately agreed as fabric walls and gold spray paint seemed effortless and economical to me.

One morning, I got a panicked phone call from Jon who said, "Richard, you'll never believe it, but *vandals* broke into the office and spray-painted the office gold." Beyond the decor, I laughed, calmed him down, and told him we now had a designer office. As far as decorating the space went, Jon and I found an old wooden desk on the street in the garbage and hauled it up for our first employee, Julie Paciulli, who was our finance person. We literally opened a closet, put the desk in there, turned on the closet light, and voilà—a private office was born. I had this idea to get an old dining room table and put it in the conference room. Marc picked out velvet gold-and-wood Napoleonic chairs. One day, I came into a new client meeting that Jon had set up. He also told me he ordered lunch. Even though Jon was newly married, he was still in "fraternity mode" and had ordered a pizza pie with some soda and beer. After the meeting, I complained in my usual fashion, and Jon threw his hands up. "What's wrong? You didn't like the pizza?" I immediately took over lunch and promptly went to my local Long Island thrift store and found an old china service and real silver. It was a truly Oscar/Felix moment.

The office had attitude and energy and was young, young, young—everyone was either twenty or twenty-one. It took on a huge amount of an insane energy when the staff started Rollerblading through the space—and often colliding with clients. You could tell there was a cultural frisson and something wonderful was going to happen. One day, an older client was standing in the reception area when a young intern raced in on a skateboard and knocked him over. As he was dusting himself off, another employee knocked into him on Rollerblades! "Is everyone in this agency on wheels?!" he yelled.

About this time, I read Jerry Della Femina's now classic book on advertising, *From the Wonderful Folks Who Brought You Pearl Harbor.* In it, Jerry wrote about the time his fledgling agency almost went out of business until he had the idea to throw a party, which actually helped them get some new business. Not knowing Jerry, we decided to barter an agency party at our new client, the restaurant Positano on Park Avenue South. (We did an ad for them there, which read "Finally, an authentic Italian restaurant where no one's been shot. Yet.") Taking a page from Jerry's playbook, I also decided to invite Jerry. And to make a long story short, not only did Jerry come, but he also became a friend and my mentor. Not to mention it was a great party, and we also picked up some new biz between cocktails! The press we cleverly invited suddenly became interested in us.

The first article on us, entitled "Hot Copy," ran in *New York Magazine,* and the telephone started ringing and business meetings started happening. About that time, potential clients would call up and say, "I have two or three million dollars to spend, not as much as Kenneth Cole" (which at the time was far more than his budget). Clearly, people thought he was spending more because of the buzz and attention our first ad campaign received. Jon and I started calling this the "multiplier effect," i.e., if you were a small client with a million dollars, we could multiply it and make it look like you were spending five or ten, based on the breakthrough campaign and cumulative PR. In new business, Jon displayed an amazing energy, and an unrelenting and sharp-as-a-knife drive. Like a great boxer, Jon could go more rounds than anyone I'd met before. And when paired with great creative it was an undeniable combo.

Another great example of the multiplier effect was the "No Excuses" blockbuster campaign that we created with Donna Rice for Kenneth's brother, Neil. Their father, Charles Cole, had created Candies, and both brothers would follow in his footsteps (excuse the pun). No Excuses was a great name for an eighties jeans company, and lightning struck twice when we hired Gary Hart's "monkey business" paramour, Donna Rice.

The commercial was one long pan of the jeans with Donna saying to camera, "I don't make excuses. I just wear them."

It may be hard to comprehend, but this was all pre-Paris, pre-Britney, pre-Lindsay. Being in the eye of the storm with "the scandal magnet of the moment" was actually surreal. What was I, twenty-six? And we gave an actual *press conference* to introduce the campaign! I can still feel the glare of the popping flashbulbs. The press corps surrounded the building where we had Donna holed up, and shooting her seemed like a scene out of a movie. Once the commercial was shot, edited, and in the can, we used the press conference to act as the catalyst for free press. We simply handed out tapes to the press. The news stations ran the commercial as news—which became free media—and suddenly every client with a small budget wanted a piece of that.

It would be hard to follow up with the next No Excuses girl, and we weirdly hired Joan Rivers after her battle with Johnny Carson, her show's cancellation, and her husband's suicide. Joan, who was fairly sad at the time (an understatement), was also painfully thin, and I remember the stylist having to use clothes pins on her jeans legs to affect a good fit. The copy for the commercial actually had Joan saying, "If these jeans look that good on someone like me, can you imagine what they'd do for your body—little tramp!"

Dari Marder (Neil's director of advertising and PR), me, Joan Rivers, and Neil Cole

Joan liked the gig, and we clicked as I knew we would, and she invited me to write some comedy for her. She reminded me a bit of my mentor, Lois, and when I was in LA, I went to hear Joan try out her act in some of the small LA clubs. I remember getting paid a few dollars a joke and that I sold a few Michael Jackson and Princess Stephanie jokes before I realized that the margin of being a comedy writer had nothing on the ad biz. Still, it was fun, and I honed my craft being able to think and write in someone else's distinct voice.

It's no surprise that all of us at kbp wanted a more liberal, socially conscious-based world, and perhaps it was totally subconscious that the first famous campaigns the agency became noted for also took politicians down a notch. The Kenneth Cole campaign ads featuring characters like Imelda Marcos, Dan Quayle, and Oliver North captured the public's attention, as it hadn't seen this kind of creativity in the advertising business before. Under Dan Quayle's picture all we said was "Don't forget to vot," a great play on his not knowing how to spell potato by spelling it potatoe. The ad we did featuring Oliver North's picture had the caption "Isn't it time America focused less on arms and more on feet?" All of which generated news story after news article.

We were hiring the best and the brightest—young talent who all wanted to be part of our renegade culture. It was incredibly fun getting up in the morning and coming to work. You never knew who was going to call or what was going to happen. One bright day, I walked outside my office (I was filling it with lunch boxes—cheap decor) when the receptionist (an intern who was wearing a paper bag over his head like the unknown comic—no one blinked an eye at this) said, "Richard, there's someone on the phone for you. Some governor?"

Yeah, right, I thought. I picked up the phone but then heard this distinct southern accent.

"Hi y'all, this is Governor John Y. Brown from Keeentucky. I'm traveling up to New York with my wife, Phyllis George, and we are looking for agencies for our new company, Chicken By George. We just read about y'all in *New York Magazine* and wanted to come in and say hello." After I hung up the phone, I scratched my head before letting the staff know that later that afternoon our little office would be hosting a governor and one of the country's most glamorous women: Phyllis George, Miss America and the first female sportscaster. Hmmm, I thought, what are we going to serve them?

"Could someone go and get some Pepperidge Farm cookies?" I ordered "the Milanos" (thinking that was sufficiently fancy). Thank heavens, we now had real china. "Could someone go down the hall to the washroom and clean the teacups?" I said. "In an hour or so, Miss America is showing up, and we have to look a little professional." Why I didn't tell the receptionist to take the paper bag off his head I don't know, but I thought as long as I had a Milano on a plate we were ready for anything.

We didn't realize that the stock market crash of 1987 and ABC's *20/20* were also ready to knock by the time we served tea and cookies.

A MATCH MADE IN MEDIA

Sometimes opportunity knocks and no one's home.

When *20/20* called looking to see if we had a potential client to follow us on a *behind the scenes* journey of creating a TV commercial, it was if we were under the doorframe installing the knocker. I told them the governor and Miss America were in the office the day before and then I told the governor and Miss America that *20/20* was looking for an interested client. Did I say "no brainer"? We got the account and a commitment from *20/20*.

One of the first people we hired, once we knew we were going to be on national television with the *20/20* piece, was my former art director at JWT, Marisa Acocella. When I first met Marisa, I thought she was incredibly cool and talented—part Carrie Bradshaw and part Anjelica Huston. I remember calling Marisa on the phone and the conversation went something like this:

"Hi, babe."

"Hi, babe. How's it hanging over at kbp?"

"Great, want to be on national television? *20/20* is doing a piece on us and Miss America, and we need a real art director."

"Can't wait to get the #$@% out of here. When do I start?"

"When can you be here?"

Marisa immediately jumped ship and came over as one of our founding partners.

Phyllis and the governor had this new company called Chicken By George, which was a line of marinated chicken breasts in different flavors they'd concocted in their Kentucky kitchen. The governor's Kentucky Fried Chicken pedigree and Phyllis's beauty and wholesomeness seemed a match made in chicken. Jon, Marisa, and I traveled down to their gorgeous, stately home in Lexington called Cave Hill Place, and I still remember the scented candles, the fire cracking in the great room, and Phyllis's amazing quilt collection. She cooked up her chicken cutlets for us, which were as good as anything my grandma Anna ever made or you could get at Woodro's. So I was impressed.

Hormel and other food companies had been interested in Chicken By George, and the PR, TV shoot, and buzz was a seemingly smart way to build the brand and perhaps attract more buyers. Certainly the governor had made a fortune with KFC, and this was going to prove to be a tasty morsel as well. Phyllis, who is gorgeous, has a very funny and self-deprecating personality. As I got to know her, I would always tell her how funny she was, and it seemed even funnier to me that she seemed a bit shocked by it. Anyway, in typical kbp fashion, Marisa and I presented this commercial in which Phyllis looked over her shoulder at the camera in a backless evening gown and would say something like (this was twenty-five years ago), "Hi, I'm Phyllis George, and I'm here to show America something they've never seen before. My breasts." And then she would turn (and since the dress was backless, you thought she was gong to be naked), but instead, she would be wearing a halter gown and holding up two packages of Chicken By George. "My chicken breasts, that is."

Phyllis loved the commercial and loved acting it out for unsuspecting friends and acquaintances. She got a great laugh out of it, but I don't think Governor Brown did because it was apparent he wasn't buying that one! However, he quickly approved the tag line "The First Lady of Chicken," since, technically, Phyllis was indeed the First Lady of Kentucky and had achieved a few firsts: the first woman sportscaster, not to mention the first Miss America to take a spill on the runway.

Spending time with Phyllis and the governor was really a trip. A trip to the South, that is. The governor, with his lilting southern accent and shock of white hair, carried a big black briefcase that held all sorts of entrepreneurial deals (which reminded me of a carpetbag). He was a real Southern entrepreneur in every sense and would throw lots of ideas at us, which always seemed to emerge from that bottomless black bag, like, "What do you think of this idea, boys? My good friend Keeeny?" Then he'd block out the idea "Keeeny Rogers Roasters" or "Kenny Rogers Twenty-Minute Martinizing" with his hands.

The governor knew politics and chicken and wanted his wife filmed in the best possible light. Marisa and I came up with a number of concepts but eventually landed on a sweet commercial of Phyllis descending a grand staircase.

Where we ended up wasn't exactly breakthrough, but it was something appropriate for a governor and Miss America. And besides being our first location shoot, it was also being filmed concurrently by the *20/20* crew.

Phyllis, me, Marisa, and the producer, Deborah

Within weeks, we flew out to Los Angeles where Phyllis secured a location from her friend (a well-known plastic surgeon) who had a grand mansion in Holmby Hills. It sort of looked like the house the Clampetts (from *The Beverly Hillbillies*) lived in. Phyllis took a bungalow at the

Beverly Hills Hotel, and despite the small budget, Marisa and I got to stay at the hotel as well. One day, Marisa and I went up to the Holmby Hills house to location scout for the commercial. I was poking around in the living room looking at photos of the plastic surgeon: a one-time model and actor who had a myriad of silver-framed black-and-white photos of himself with all the major stars: Marilyn Monroe, Rita Hayworth, and Cary Grant, to name a few.

"Can I help you?" a voice bellowed through the marble foyer.

"Oh, we're here scouting for the commercial for Phyllis George."

"Oh, yes," the handsome, tall, sandy-haired man said as he looked me up and down. He was standing next to three people, all in dark sunglasses.

"I'm the owner. This is Mrs. Johnny Carson," he said flatly. "This is my daughter, Irene. And *this* is my lover, Stephen."

"How do you do. I'm Richard and this is Marisa."

"Welcome to Hollyweird," Marisa whispered, and kicked me.

The day of the shoot arrived, and it felt surreal to be filming the commercial and being filmed, at the same time (again, all this was before reality television). Phyllis was a dream to work with and looked gorgeous on camera. She did a number of costume changes in good grace even though her custom Vicky Tiel gowns had been late to arrive, having been stuck at LAX. My favorite moment occurred after the first day of shooting. Marisa, Phyllis, and I drove into Fatburger for a late snack, and once in possession of her Fatbuger, Phyllis waved her hand at me before she took a bite of her burger. "Look away y'all," she declared.

"Why?" I said, not quite understanding.

"It's not BQ!

"BQ?" I shook my head

"Beauty queen. It's not BQ. A lady never lets a man see her eating a Fatburger."

Now I understood. I looked away. But although I honored her request, I really did want to see how a beauty queen handled a burger. "Look away, y'all," she declared again as she saw me starting to peek. I never did get to see it!

The shoot was so much fun. Marisa and I were like two kids in a candy shop, eating and drinking at The Polo Lounge and also lounging by the pool whenever we had a free moment, soaking up the Beverly Hills lifestyle. Marisa had also been obsessed with Stephen (the homeowner's twenty-something buff lover), and the next day over the lunch break, she approached him as he was sitting alone eating a turkey sandwich. "So, Stephen," Marisa said in a leading tone, "you live here or what?" Stephen, who was about our age at the time, just looked at her forlornly between bites and said, "You know, when I first moved to LA, I always looked at these big houses from the outside and wondered who lived there beyond the walls and the gates."

"And?" Marisa said somewhat lasciviously.

"And now that I'm here, I just want to get the hell out!"

Ellen Rossen, the *20/20* producer, was eager to get behind-the-scenes dirt, but having secured a celebrity, a mansion, and a hot, young agency, she still seemed a bit disappointed, I thought. This was as clean as an Ivory campaign. Phyllis may have regaled us with stories about her short-lived marriage to Robert Evans, but none of that was available for the camera, and I think that they were a bit let down by the final script and commercial. That said, a politician and a Miss America weren't going to do anything less then squeaky clean. Not that they would; that's who they were. As Phyllis always said, they were "white picket fence, church on Sundays."

After the commercial wrapped and Phyllis, the governor, and their assistant, Dee, packed up all the couture and Phyllis's jewelry cases and went back to Kentucky, Marisa and I spent a luxurious day by the BHH pool, having chopped salad and tanning. Marisa came up with the idea that we should call the owner of the mansion and invite him out for a thank-you lunch. To this day, I'm convinced that somebody wiretapped the pool at the BHH: When Marisa called him and invited him, he said he'd heard we'd been talking about him at the pool (and he repeated, word for word, the entire conversation), and since it was a Monday, no one was there! He did accept our invitation nonetheless, and the lunch proved to be an eye-opener. Marisa kept kicking me under the table at every bit of juicy gossip. He wanted to go to L'Orangerie, which, at the time, had a very Betsy Bloomingdale–Nancy Reagan–Bel Air ladies-who-lunch vibe. Of course, Betsy was there and said hello to our lunch guest. Over lunch, our man in Hollywood gave us a rare peek into his world.

"I was married twice, but I was always a yo-yo," he said over a martini.

"What's a yo-yo?" I asked naïvely.

"I went with women *and* men!"

Marisa kicked me yet again under the table in the shins. She really did give me black-and-blue marks! "In the 1930s," he reminisced, "I was discovered as a male model and sent to this dentist to have my teeth done. He did things to me when I was under the gas, and when I went to Hollywood, he gave me Cary's number."

"Cary?"

"Cary Grant. He was living with Randolph Scott at the time. We become lovers."

"Cary Grant?" I almost fell over.

Over lunch, he ticked off a number of leading men and women he'd been with. By the time lunch was over, he was up to Rita Hayworth. "After she was divorced from Aly. She was divine. We did the rhumba under the stars in Saint-Jean-Cap-Ferrat."

Needless to say, my first shoot in Los Angeles was quite interesting. In many ways, having this reality TV–style experience early on paved the way for us to be more risk-taking, experimental, and open. Many agencies or agency people are terrified of letting people behind the curtain, thus either turning down interesting and provocative opportunities or becoming controlling at the prospect. Negotiating the public, along with the public and the private lives of the people I have worked with, has helped craft the DNA of our agency and our open work philosophy. Interestingly, all these years later, on Monday, I just saw a screening of Morgan Spurlock's newest movie *The Greatest Movie Ever Sold* at Sony. Morgan, a superb documentary filmmaker who made the Academy Award–nominated documentary *Supersize Me*, approached me last year to help him secure a client for his newest documentary about marketing, where he sells off sponsorships to pay for and promote the whole movie. The movie (which is hilarious) documents his journey to find and secure these sponsors. The first quarter of the movie details all the agency executives and brands who turn him down on his quest until I help him land his first brand, Ban deodorant. It had been hard to get a client involved because clients are inherently nervous when they don't have control, but I told Morgan, "Once you get the first client, the rest will follow." Once Ban deodorant came on board, the rest did follow. In many ways, I'm not sure if 20/20 and Phyllis hadn't come along that I would have been as open to all the future possibilities both real and ridiculous. While it may be almost twenty years later, the same issues come into play when the cameras roll behind the scenes. No matter how you look at it, whether it's a Miss America or a documentary filmmaker, advertising intrigues the public, and sometimes peeling back the curtain provides an interesting view. It's not only funny, but it's provocative, crazy, and ridiculous. It can also be a match made in media. When it's right.

CHAPTER FIVE
MY MOST UN-FAVORITE YEAR

THAT YEAR, 1988, WAS A year the proverbial shit hit the fan. The *20/20* full-length segment and the covers of various industry magazines were just a part of it. The twelve months that unfurled also saw my mother's death from a heart attack, my father's surgery for a benign brain tumor, and almost a year to the date of my father's surgery, a bomb threat in the office. From the outside, the business success looked great, but I felt like I was in a blender on purée. In the Jewish tradition, one sits shivah for a parent, which is a week of mourning solitude, praying, and remembrance in one's home. (It's sort of like a wake but more food and less alcohol.) I do remember getting a call from a client I still know quite well who commented that his service had "been slipping" the week I was out. Given that we had only a few employees, it wasn't too hard to figure out that it wouldn't be a banner week. I saw a different side to people during this time, both positive and negative.

The thing that struck me the most was that it all felt so surreal. I mean Marilyn (a.k.a. Maude) had a huge presence sweeping into rooms, delivering a bon mot, and disappearing to call her sister, Aunt Jackie, on the telephone. There was often laughter, chatter, and a bit of screaming in the house, so the silence was particularly strange and disturbing.

I truly loved and adored her, and she passed away at such a young

69

age (she was only fifty-six). She never got to meet my wonderful wife, Dana, or our three children, but she did get to read that first article on the agency, "Hot Copy" in *New York Magazine,* that generated so much of our initial business. I think she would have been proud.

As I look back on my mother's death that year, I was so young, I almost didn't know how to process all that was happening during that period of time. Of course, I cried a great deal but tried to get through it for the sake of my dad, who seemed lost. While I went back to work the following week, nothing felt quite right. The mourning process was too fresh, and I didn't know whether I was coming or going; I couldn't place my bearings. Work was a great anchor, and I plowed most of my time and energy into it.

I had no choice, actually. After a year or two of growth, we already started to outgrow our first space at 1133 Broadway. We looked for and eventually found a new space and landed on a building on lower Sixth Avenue, across from a park and next to a vocational high school. The neighborhood had been fairly mom-and-pop Italian with little restaurants, but for the most part it was pretty much no man's land. Twenty-three years later, there's an Aveda and a Starbucks across the street, and The Donald just finished Trump Soho around the corner. I always say follow the artists and/or young people, and a neighborhood will grow.

For our new space, we hired a young, talented architect named Peter Guzy. He created a *real* agency look with a glass-enclosed conference room and offices, and a studio on the perimeter. It felt incredibly grown-up and glamorous. And at times, being only twenty-seven, I felt like I was playing at being a boss, too. The office hadn't lost its youthful, fun energy, and I had two stamps made, one of a smiley face in blue and one of a frowning face in red. Each day, I would stamp all the proposed ads, and the creative people actually loved getting a smiley face and a "Love Love Love" handwritten from me when they presented good creative work. We operated on gut and were incredibly un-PC. When the Rob Lowe sex video came out, we thought nothing of getting a copy and doing a screening. This sense of optimism and joie de vivre showed up in the six-page *New York Magazine* article entitled "The Ad Brats."

The Ad Brats arrive on the scene

Jon and I were photographed against multiple lightbulbs, and I had on my Charivari Yohji blazer (another story) and green cowboy boots (which became my trademark). All I can say is that when the article broke (and this was before the Internet, so people still really *read* magazines), it mentioned I was single, and women sent underwear (new and a used thong), and the phone kept ringing. We were really on our way, despite a deranged stalker who saw the article and called me, pretending to be Demi Moore. I had to call celebrity security maven Gavin de Becker to help me on that one.

Due to the press, "The Ad Brats" moniker stuck. I guess when you're in your twenties and start a successful enterprise, the press needs to find a way to rationalize it or take you down a notch. That said, we were good copy, providing sound bites such as "You're nobody until somebody hates you" and "I could sell pork at a bar mitzvah!" When you're young and don't have much to lose you can say whatever you want. Even the *New York Times* reporter at the time, Phil Dougherty, wrote, "I have socks older than those guys." In the *New York Magazine* article, our Charivari client Jon Weiser was quoted as saying, "They're so young, it's disgusting." We were so young to be running a new business that routinely, before a new business pitch, my partner, Jon, would try to put talcum powder in his hair to give him a bit of gray at the temples (it only looked like he had dandruff), and I wore glasses to appear older as well (pictures now reveal that I just looked like Mr. Potato Head). The ad brat thing was on one hand a great way to get people interested in us, but while it piqued people's interest, their expectations were that Jon and I would be totally rude and obnoxious in person (which was quite far from the truth). It was always surprising to people when their low expectations were raised by mature and gracious behavior. (They didn't know I was one of the few men who was brought up the by Marilyn [a.k.a. Maude] to write handwritten thank-you notes.) Or that Jon was perfecting his client golf game!

Eventually, it became important for us to impart good manners to the staff who, for the most part, had bought into the bratty, rebellious image and thought they "should act that way" when they became a kbp employee. Every so often, we would interview a clean-cut preppy account person who, once they got the job, showed up the next day unshaven in a leather jacket, virtually swinging from the "chandies" as my friend Jamie always says. It even happened with an older new business guy, Ken Glazer, who was in his late fifties at the time he worked with us. He was a conservative married guy. One day, he was wearing a suit; the next day, he showed up at the agency with a ponytail and an earring. We had to take him aside and said, "Ken, you don't have to dress that way. We like you just the way you are!"

In fact, the ad brat culture and bad manners taught everyone a good lesson and resulted in us *not* getting or having the ability to get one of the world's best accounts. In the advertising business, there is a tendency for people to earn ad dollars as assistants or freelancing while pursuing other careers at the same time. Everyone is something else or wants to be. He's not a copywriter; he's an aspiring filmmaker. She's not a junior account executive but a conceptual artist, and so forth. Anyway, we had this lovely receptionist who was also an opera singer, and perhaps her mind was on Verdi and not on the phones.

I'd flown out to Seattle with one of the partners to have a meeting with a wonderful new company we were hearing great things about and its founder. When we arrived at the company headquarters, the founder's assistant took us aside and explained that the meeting was canceled. Canceled!? We'd flown all the way to the left coast and not the *sunny* part! How could they cancel it when we had traveled all that way and I couldn't even go to the beach? She explained that when she had called our offices to confirm the meeting, our receptionist had put her on hold and also had been incredibly rude. When the founder found out about it, he canceled the meeting and said "rude receptionist, rude company." We were crestfallen. Needless to say, the founder was Howard Schultz and the company was Starbucks! And Howard was right. We flew back to New York empty-handed and had a chat with the staff. I had a literal example of the power of being polite, particularly on the phone with a secretary or a receptionist: We got the Kenneth Cole account, in part, because his fun assistant took a liking to me on the phone, and when Kenneth didn't want to see us—she got us through the door. So in the end, while he never knew it, Howard influenced more than just the culture of Starbucks.

Indeed, in the advertising business, having a great assistant with great manners actually is like having a secretary of state: They are your ambassador and your face to the world. People underestimate assistants, but having started out as one, I can tell you that good ones can tell what client is "real" by how they get along with the client's assistant. Great assistants—like Carol, who has worked with me for more than sixteen years—always have more insight and power than people know. They are an executive's first line of defense and the more successful an executive, the better the executive's assistant. I am always suspect of people who go through assistants like tissue paper because it definitely signifies there is an issue.

Speaking of behavior, Carol and I are *old school* when it comes to professional interactions. Calls are returned, flowers are sent for a birthday or anniversary, and thank-you notes are still handwritten and stamped with real stamps (not an agency postage machine). I speak from experience when I say that while being young and brash is fun, it very often loses you a star account. One can still be innovative, and on the cutting edge, but gentlemanly. That not only makes you a star but helps rake in the bucks! Take it from me. That one morning when we arrived sleepless in Seattle, we missed our morning coffee altogether.

The ad brat thing was having too big a cultural impact on the company. From then on, we made a conscious shift to hire only smart, nice, and well-mannered people, and change our public image. For many years, I would say, I had to also retrain creative folk who were brought up in the industry being told that creative integrity was "fighting for the work." I quickly dispelled this notion and said, "We don't fight with our clients. Fighting gets you nowhere or fired." I generally always admired the clients and have never taken them for granted. After all, they pay our bills and are often lovely people to boot. Sometimes I had to discipline a young creative who was out of line, but the clients always knew that we were on their side. Now, I'm not suggesting there aren't times when you need to make an impassioned plea to a client to buy an out-of-the-box idea or innovative work—but you wanted to *persuade* them as opposed to *fight* with them. Here's one of my favorite examples of this talent.

Andy and Carrie Kozinn owned a wonderful suit manufacturing company, Saint Laurie Merchants Tailors. The company was truly unique and offered the finest tailoring at a lower price point, since they owned the loft building and therefore had lower production costs and rent. Andy and Carrie were enormously proud of their third-generation family business housed in a fabulous turn-of-the-century warehouse building on Lower Broadway.

In order to communicate style and price, I came up with a simple ad. A few years earlier, I had started collecting photography (Alterna-Dad and I always give each other a black-and-white photo for our birthdays, thanks to his introducing me to this art form). I was greatly influenced by the elegant, iconic portraits of Horst, who shot the greats of his day, like Chanel and Noël Coward, often posed in gorgeous suits and looking chic, dangling a cigarette.

I proposed a black-and-white image of an aristocratic-looking young man in a fabulous Saint Laurie suit smoking a cigarette, with the head-line "Dress British. Think Yiddish." I presented the ad to Andy, who was Jewish, and Carrie, who wasn't. I think they had trepidation since the meaning is both positive and negative (I, of course, thought it meant *smart, not cheap*). Andy firmly turned down the ad because of the con-troversial implications. The talented, young copywriter I discovered, Andy Spade, came up with a wonderful alternative with the headline, "The look is Ralph Lauren. The price is Ralph Kramden." Every meet-ing, when we presented our work, we would pull out the "Dress British" ad and urge them to run it. It finally became a running joke.

Andy Spade is and was an original. When he first came for an inter-view, he looked like he was a preppy twelve-year-old with a bow tie and Hush Puppies. And he still does. He was a junior writer at Benton & Bowles at the time, but his portfolio, although not well art-directed, was filled with fun and witty headlines. You could just tell he had *it*. It was no surprise when Andy and his then girlfriend/fiancée, Kate, started their handbag lines, Kate Spade and Jack Spade, a few years later, out of our offices. I remember looking at their first iconic fabric bag samples. No one was surprised that it became such a hit, and no one was surprised when his funny brother, David, joined the cast of *Saturday Night Live* and became famous, too. That's because the Spades have a unique sense of humor and take on the world. Their voice: The post-suburban take on culture hit a nerve and made a real dent in the zeitgeist and in fashion.

After all the joking around, Andy Kozinn informed us one day that he was making a noble decision. He was donating a kidney to his brother. After the surgery, we called Carrie to see how Andy was and she said, "Guys, you'll never believe it. As they were wheeling Andy on the gurney down to the operating theater, I told him I loved him and asked him if there was anything he wanted. He turned to me and said, 'Carrie, I love you. RUN THE AD!'"

The "Dress British" ad ran in *New York Magazine* and immediately garnered a huge amount of attention for Saint Laurie and for the agency. It only served to cement our images as enfants terribles and gave the agency a "hot" halo. To quote *New York Magazine*, the title of our first article (the one Marilyn got to read) was "Hot Copy," and it was coming off the presses daily, molten hot! The ability to talk to consumers in a bold, new way prefigured social networking, where now consumers actually control the conversation about brands and have honest and controversial conversations about a company's brand preferences.

When people ask me what I'm most proud of, I am proud that we brought such a fresh and modern tone and voice to the advertising business with our copy. Much like my Long G'Island accent, our copy and perspective had freshness to it from day one because of its honesty (which people still remember from the Kenneth Cole ads). Having been raised in the superlatives of Brandpa's world, everything was or had to be "new and improved" or "buy one get one free"—bold introductory phrases that were meant to appeal to children and people who had a base level of intelligence.

Kbp's combination of honesty, humor, and a New York "telling it like it is" boldness seemed to rock the industry. When paired with our creative director Bill Oberlander's elegant art direction, we labeled the combination "the brass fist in the velvet glove." Headlines like, "Finally, an authentic Italian restaurant where no one's been shot. Yet." for Positano Restaurant on Park Avenue South or "The only way you can get higher is illegal." for Jump sneakers broke through. Clients liked it and the phone kept ringing.

Twenty-four years later, the phone is still ringing off the hook, I think also, in part, because our attitude—and work ethic—from day one was doing whatever it took to solve clients' problems—even when we had no full comprehension of what that meant. We wanted to get the business and, more importantly, we wanted the work to not only be creative but to actually *work*. Many creative people really feel they are accountable to the "creative community," which is made up of critics who can often display a certain level of creative snobbery. But it is also made up of others who don't come to play this game and don't care about the results. I have always felt an obligation to the hardworking "families" (staff members) of our clients who want to be proud of the public face of our advertising, hence proud of the company and brand they work for.

One experience I had illustrates this with surgical precision. It was 2008. I was walking through a sea of polyester. Gray-haired, solid, kindly faces in powder blue jackets and diminutive blonde women in high heels, all wearing name tags, parted around me. I saw people furtively glance at me. They whispered. A few stared. I knew they knew that I wasn't one of *them*. Maybe the long hair was the giveaway, or the lemon yellow European blazer. Either way, they'd pegged me from the start. They knew I was the *other*.

I was an ad agency creative person.

Only months before, kbp had gotten the smaller part of the advertising assignment for this client. Our agency wasn't in charge of the overall campaign but of a smaller part of the business. But as luck would have it, the large global ad agency that had beat us out for the main part of the business had struck out. So right before the holidays, the client turned to us, and we'd worked as a committed team all through our Christmas break to come up with a new advertising campaign to help restore their confidence—and their brand. We'd shot, locked, and loaded the commercials in record time, and the client asked us to introduce the new campaign to their franchisee group at the convention.

I'd only spoken in front of five hundred people once or twice. I found it a nerve-racking experience. As I looked at the huge monitors filling the mammoth room in the Orlando Convention Center, I gulped. How could I possibly get up in front—of not five hundred people—but something like five thousand? I wasn't a celebrity or a politician, but there I was, getting ready to speak to five thousand franchisees and introduce the new campaign for Wendy's.

I had one bit of solace. I knew they would love it. We were bringing back the Wendy character, herself, after a thirty-five-year ad hiatus, and we were introducing a line they would also love: "It's waaaay better than fast food. It's Wendy's."

The client had locked Jon and I away for two full days to practice with teleprompters, monitors, and coaches. Although we were in Florida, we hadn't seen the sunshine or felt the humidity in days. It was blasting cold from the industrial air-conditioning, and Jon and I rewrote our scripts and practiced again and again. . . . Jon's father had been an actor, so thankfully it was in Jon's genes, and he was less nervous opening first. The day of reckoning arrived, and Kerri Anderson, the president and CEO of Wendy's, came out onstage and introduced us as their new agency after being honest about some negative results regarding the prior agency's campaign. The group wasn't happy, and they were fairly intimidating. As we walked up to the stage, I went through the old game of trying to imagine everyone in their underwear, but the thought of five thousand boxers, briefs, and brassieres only scared me more.

I looked out into the endless sea of faces while Jon finished his opening, and I knew it was time for me to do it. "Well," I said, "I guess it's not hard to figure out who's the creative one." I laughed. There was a pause. And then the audience broke into laughter and applause. I knew I was home free. Still, I couldn't believe that I was standing in front of five thousand people, introducing a national campaign for one of America's leading fast-food brands, when only a few years before, I was answering phones, a receptionist working for free, and then for a nine-thousand-dollar-a-year salary.

As I turned toward the monitor, I caught a glimpse of myself introducing the new tagline, "It's waaaay better than fast food. It's Wendy's," and the audience leaped to their feet, cheering in a standing ovation. A warm feeling spread all over me. I knew that despite the fact that I'd chosen an industry my relatives didn't quite understand or that some of my neighbors thought was frivolous, Jon and I had helped solve a business issue for thousands of hardworking small business people. The franchisees were proud of their work and their brand again. They were proud of me, despite my Barry Gibb shag. And Jon and I and our team were so proud of the business. After all, other than a car account, there is nothing as billable as a fast food account. And I had a flashback to eating Wendy's fries and having a Frosty in our first office; just the two of us and a typewriter sending out our first bill. . . .

CHAPTER SIX
I ALMOST DID IT MY WAY

ADVERTISING PEOPLE BY NATURE TEND to be quirky, fun, and loquacious, as it is, and I've had the pleasure of working with some of the more interesting people over the years. I've often said running a creative department in an ad agency is like overseeing a kindergarten class *and* a zoo. You have to balance being disciplined and also have a very liberal hand. After all, you're dealing with creative people, not accountants. They're never on time; they don't do time sheets. They might not come in if they're depressed. They might smoke too much or drink too much or have other vices. Sometimes it's shepherding the lost; other times it's cracking down on a free-for-all and making sure things don't get too out of hand. I once knew an older guy who ran an agency and was so upset that his staff didn't show up on time in the morning, he stood at the entrance with a pocket watch, clocking everyone in. The first day, people were scared and took him seriously. After that, he would just wait with his watch as no on bothered to come in. I could have told him that if he wanted to clock his staff, he should have run an assembly line in Detroit, not an ad agency.

One thing is for sure, it's never boring. I have to say as my grandma Elsie said, "Take the best and leave the rest." You have to get the best out of the people by inspiring them to do their best. No idea is a bad idea, and you have to embrace all the craziness, lateness included. I once hired a creative guy who photographed himself in situ having sex with his girlfriend (the doggy position). While I was on the fence about his work, I knew he would take creative risks, so I hired him. The only time it works against you and the person is when their hobby becomes a frustrated career move, i.e., the writer who wants to be a director or the account person who wants to be a screenwriter, and can't. They usually end up with unrealistic expectations and may leave the business only to return or freelance in worse shape than when they were on a successful trajectory.

As a business owner, one also has to keep a healthy distance from office shenanigans and office politics. I only broke my rule once about dating someone in the office when I was single and she was a freelancer. Even though it wasn't serious, I held back because I thought it wasn't a good move. There's nothing worse than a boss who cheats or runs around with his employees, and I do not recommend it. The one time I did break this rule was actually a *complete surprise.*

I take a sleeping pill when I fly, and I always need a few hours to wake up and smell the coffee. It was a particularly bumpy flight, and I took a higher dosage than normal. The next morning, I woke up and voilà! There was a young woman, who worked for me, *in my bed,* in a black negligee doing lovely things to me. Since I really had no idea when I woke up, I was just glad she was attractive! (Yes, Dana, when I was single.)

That said, I have always kept a distance from the "goings on" in the office. And like the client who called me when he got wind of his account guy dancing in a g-string at a strip club, I replied, "Everyone has multiple talents at kbp, and that's why we hired him!"

*   *   *   *

I firmly believe that in times of economic crisis, fun—especially as it relates to the advertising or creative businesses—is even more of a currency than ever. Creating a culture of fun and innovation leads to breakthroughs. Most traditional organizations (and I've worked with many) understand this to a point and try to institutionalize *moments* of fun through an away day or a holiday party, but those moments can be forced and fleeting. Most of all, creating a fun and innovative culture starts with the leadership, and if they can't laugh at themselves, I can assure you there ain't going to be a whole lot of laughs making the rounds.

My wildly amusing (and amused) former creative director, Marisa, comes from an incredibly warm and loving Italian-American family. Her mother, Violetta, is one of the best cooks I know (the most incredible Christmas dinners with Aunt Mary . . . mmm, eggplant rollatini). She even showed up on a Reynolds Wrap shoot (when we were working at Thompson) and gave her opinion. She walked right over to the client and the photographer, stopped the shoot, and said, "I think you need to shoot the food on a doily! Everything looks better on a doily."

Clearly, like her daughter, Violetta was not a wilting flower. After the *20/20* segment "How to Create a Commercial" aired about Phyllis George's chicken line, Chicken By George, in 1987, Violetta called Marisa and me at the office. We gathered around the phone waiting to hear Violetta kvell about her daughter and the piece. After all, how many times do you get to see your daughter on national television?

"So what did you think, Mom?" Marisa asked, waiting for her approval.

"What I think is that the two of you need to get nose jobs. You two had the biggest noses on television."

I kid you not! And then she added, "Maybe you can both go in for a two-for-one special."

Like Streisand, Marisa never did get her nose fixed and clearly neither did I, but we all had a great laugh. And still do. Marisa has always been something of a provocateur. I'll never forget when we presented work to Randy Jones, the then conservative publisher of *Esquire*. Marisa went over, sat on his lap, and sang "Happy Birthday, Mr. President" à la Monroe, since it was his birthday. Marisa has one of the best senses of humor I know, and she went on to become a well-regarded *New Yorker* cartoonist (after I introduced her to Grace Mirabella, who immediately saw her talent with cartoons like "Fendi Bag Lady"). She even turned her fight with breast cancer into the *New York Times* bestselling humorous graphic novel *Cancer Vixen,* which was recently optioned by Cate Blanchett, who is set to play Marisa in the upcoming movie. Marisa also went on to marry Silvano Marchetto, who owns the famous and esteemed restaurant Da Silvano. I eat there virtually every day for lunch.

I hit the jackpot, given one of my best friends and forever colleagues married one of New York's most famous restaurateurs. Hello, *melanzane alla parmigiana*!

Having the ability to laugh at yourself also allows people to laugh *with* you and not at you. Life at kbp couldn't have been more fun through the years, and the only pressure we lived under was self-imposed. Culturally, we also decided to institute our *own* version of what other agencies or businesses did with a customized reward system. If other agencies had an executive golf getaway in Phoenix, we invented Camp Day, where we rented out a camp and bussed everyone in for color war. Perhaps our most well-known take on corporate America was not to just have an awards ceremony or employee-of-the-month but to rock it kbp-style. Our Oscars (for the best work) wasn't a serious trophy but The Golden Bagel! The best and brightest were nominated for this award by first winning the golden cruller in order to be eligible for The Golden Bagel. Why? Because everyone knows a cruller is not as good as a bagel. Today the golden bagels are realistic-looking, spray-painted plastic bagels. But way back, when we weren't smart enough, we spray-painted and laminated *real* bagels, which were noshed on by real New York City mice and rats when everyone went home at night.

Since kbp also has always had many international employees, we did many things that were not just "New York." And we always encouraged them to add to our culture. We hired many Brits who were dynamic and interesting, including Kiki Kendrick, who was and is an out-there artist. We lured her to kbp as an art director, and she is now a well-known actress and comedienne in London. Kiki was appalled that American ad people didn't all go to the pub after work or on Fridays. So she brought the pub to kbp. She put a British flag on a drinks trolley, put on an apron, and wheeled it around the office, mixing drinks. Even though Kiki is long gone, her trolley remains as a kbp fixture. And when people gather for "a trolley" these days, they know it's time to let off steam or hear a big announcement.

Randy Cohen and I worked together for Donny Deutsch, and many years later he ran production for us at kbp. Randy was an inherently good person with a great sense of humor. It was heartbreaking to see Randy, the father of a young girl, pass away from cancer. We held a memorial at SOB's and a trolley to honor his memory. I know Randy would have approved of the toasts, the laughter, and the tears. And the trolley!

*   *   *   *

As I said, we try to have fun by not taking ourselves too seriously. When we won the Wendy's account, Jon and I put on a red wig with pigtails to announce it to the agency. I've addressed the agency in a *Ghostbusters* suit and a dress. Our parties have always been crazy and off the charts. Every employee looks forward to the yearly boat cruise around Manhattan, and we recognize and honor the most out-there dancer. We've had the kbp prom, the kbp anniversary party (where we lit the trees with chandeliers in the park and changed the street sign to kbp Avenue—and where our male receptionist, Trevor, jumped out of a cake in a white halter gown and sang "Happy Birthday, Mr. President" to Jon and me). I had my thirtieth birthday party at Katz's Delicatessen where I hired a Borscht Belt comic who was booed off the stage, and a Chinese New Year's party at a wedding banquet hall in Chinatown. For another party, I hired Samantha Ronson before she was famous to DJ and brought in a chocolate fountain, which was an incredible hit, surprisingly, with all the anorexic models in New York. LIME, our PR and promotion subsidiary, also set up a masked fantasy room at one of our parties where the staff members were able to put on a mask and a voice simulator and discuss their office fantasies (à la reality shows). This made for a "Page Six" item, and I got called by a number of CEOs who whispered to me that they wished they were in the ad business because only *we* could get away with that.

I have always said that either an organization is driven to great results out of joy or fear. Sometimes fear works and attracts a rather masochistic group, but the results, I believe, are diminished by the dysfunction and are off-putting to truly great people. I know one well-known, successful adman that the *New York Times* reported as disciplining someone in his office by making him sit under a desk. While that might seem funny to some, it's actually tragic, in my opinion, to the firm's and owner's reputation. And to this day, I would rather walk over hot coals than be seen in his presence.

Company culture attracts the people who should be working there, and since you spend so much time at the office, it can be either painful or joyful. I choose to be around people who want to have fun. This, in turn, helps in recruitment of great talent and great ideas.

Marisa and I may have had the two biggest noses on television, but after all these years, we also laughed all the way to the bank with some great ideas and results.

*   *   *   *

The ability to have real fun makes your company and its creatives thrive. It's also what your clients want to see and feel; it's currency in a literal sense. Indeed, industry consultants have noted that fun and energy in conjunction with our work has awarded us with more new business. In the ad biz, one can't underestimate the effect of fun, flourish, and color. Clients want their ad agency owners and people to be fun and stylish. They want stories and access. They want to be entertained when they come to town (*Mad Men*, 2011 style), and they also want to break loose and have a bit of fun themselves (after they make their numbers, of course). I had an evening with Dana, which ironically always reminds me of this tenet when I think of that night.

Growing up on Long Island, Frank Sinatra was the Woody Allen of singers. What do I mean by that? Italians and Jews (and mostly everyone else) considered Ol' Blue Eyes to be their patron saint. My mother and father were huge fans since Mom was a bobby soxer in the 1940s and Dad first saw him at the Paramount when he was a "skinny marink." Since he was on Brandpa's approved list of entertainers (or *yenta-trainers* as he called it), I heard more than my fair share of "Fly Me to the Moon" and "My Way" (on the Fisher stereo around the house). I always knew if Brandpa was in a good mood, because he would whistle "Luck Be a Lady" while he was directing me by the neck and giving me whiplash (left, right) as he propelled me down Collins Avenue after dinner for a coconut patty and a photo against a painted backdrop of hand-painted palm trees that ended up in one of those magnifying key chains.

I always loved the way everyone talked about Frank as if they *knew* him. Brandpa would elbow us, wink, and say, "Did you hear what Frank said to Dean the other night?" over his veal Parmesan at Angelo's on Mulberry Street. Brandpa (and my aunt Jackie) would also keep us up-to-date on "Frankedotes," as if reporting on a son who did well. We would receive posters, magazine articles, and postcards from Florida with Frank in various poses and hats. I also got to understand musical phrasing and arrangement through Frank's TV specials and duets with Ella Fitzgerald. Frank was always generous with praise for his arrangers, like Nelson Riddle, and I understood the value of technical arrangements and phrasing.

Because of our infatuation with Frank, it's not surprising that I hear Frank in my ear every now and again when I give direction to studio technicians. Certainly, there have been times when I've scored a music track for a commercial and said (like Frank would), "We need a musical crescendo over the product portion here." Other times, I've looked for articulate voice-over reads for a radio commercial for a casino or a spreadable cheese—where I stress "benefit enunciation" like "smooth and creamy!" Every now and again, I break out *The Main Event* and thrill to Howard Cosell. If this isn't advertising and production at its best, I don't know what is! The sheer genius of the world's greatest sports announcer introducing the world's greatest legend as if it were a boxing event. That's truly conceptual advertising: Howard Cosell selling the music industry's number-one product. If you really want to know how something should be sold, break out a copy and listen and learn.

Frank could do no wrong on Long Island because even if he wasn't infallible, he also raised money for UJA and Israel and was "brothers" with Sammy Davis (liberal at the time!). Despite the fact that he went with Mia Farrow (in her boy phase), he was, well, Frank. Certainly, Brandpa loved all his dames 'cause "nobody but nobody is more gorgeous than that Ava!" Except for Grandma, of course. Although Grandma never had the *hot* factor because Brandpa preferred that she never dye her steel gray hair, he thought she was "the cat's meow" just the way she was.

A year or so after my mother died, I decided to get my father tickets to Sinatra to cheer him up. I was dating Dana and brought her along. Since I wanted Dad to have a great evening, and since it was *Frank,* I went all-out and spent a fortune for tickets at the Meadowlands. Just to give you an example of how good the seats were, we were right behind Barbara Sinatra's blonde 'do. Frank, who was in rare form, sang to Barbara, and everyone in the Garden State oohed and aahed. Every so often, Frank would take a break from a song and do his great shtick; he wiped his brow from under his Roman senator style haircut with his signature red silk pocket square.

Since we were seated so close, we could see Frank scanning the audience. He was dangling and offering his signature hankie into the crowd while crooning "Fly Me to the Moon." Dana, who was in her Ava stage with long, flowing dark tresses, surely could have been a prime candidate as he motioned the ladies to the stage. Now, you have to know that I have a few meaningful collections. Since I have been in my twenties, I have never changed my "look." I have always had a thing for cufflinks and pocket squares, and have a sizable collection of both. For some unknown and awful reason, I clamped my hand on Dana's knee as she rose to rush the stage and said, "No, don't go. Sit, Dana. Don't embarrass me." Dana looked at me like I was crazy but agreed probably because my father was there. Afterward, she said, "Richard, why did you stop me from going up and getting Frank's pocket square? I think I could've gotten it."

"I don't know," I replied. But I thought about it and realized it had to do with the insecurity people feel about one another, and what they think. I spent a few years in therapy battling this issue, and I realized (after spending a fortune) that it doesn't matter what people think. That you have to go and get what you want or you'll be the one to miss out.

When I tell people this story, they either look at me like I have three heads or completely empathize with me. It's not as if having Frank's red hankie would have changed my life, but it would have added a bit of fun and color, and I would have had a great little story to boot (i.e.,

"Remember when Frank was singing 'Fly Me to the Moon' to you, thought you looked like Ava in *The Barefoot Contessa*, and threw you his sweat-stained hankie, which just so happens to smell like a plate of appetizers at Patsy's? Well, here it is!"). And clients would have loved that story, too. Time and time again, I hear, "I love coming to visit the agency. It's the one fun thing I get to do." Some agencies, of course, do not grasp this basic concept and try to mirror their clients. That might be fine on the account side, but if the creatives aren't unique, funny, colorful, misbehaving (a bit), and throwing down a bit of a 'tude, clients aren't getting what they pay for. In fact, if I am with a client at a club or restaurant and want a better table, I use an old Sinatra trick. You take a twenty- or fifty-dollar bill, fold it into a square, and press it to the palm of the maître d' in a handshake and wink—and you always get the best seat in the house.

While that's for a client's night out, I try to no longer care about what people think, and try not to worry about being embarrassed. My only regret is not letting Dana go up and snag Frank's red *pochette*. After all, a little bit of color goes a long way.

CHAPTER SEVEN
EXPECT THE UNEXPECTED!

I THINK I WILL ALWAYS have a hard time processing being at my mother's funeral one day and being on *20/20* the next. Given all that occurred, it's not unusual I penned the line for retailer Charivari, "Expect the unexpected." Charivari was one of the first clients we landed. For those who don't know, in its day (the eighties!) it was one of the leading lights of retail. While I was never a hard-core automotive or package goods guy, I took to fashion, beauty, and luxury like a duck to water. With the rag trade in my genes, I really enjoyed the fashion clients, the models, the shoots, the stylists, and the ridiculous behavior. And I understood the importance of the retail market.

When I turned thirteen, my mother took me to Saks Fifth Avenue in Garden City (followed by a lunch of creamed chicken at Lord & Taylor) for my very stylish tan poplin bar mitzvah suit (I still have the same staple in my wardrobe). The beige platform marshmallow lace-ups were a questionable choice, yet I am sure they have found a good home in some secondhand store or on the set of *That '70s Show*. In college, when everyone was sporting designer jeans (Jordache and Calvin), I actually laminated a camp hangtag and walked around the Syracuse campus sporting Kirshenbaum Jeans. Thinking, why should someone else get play?

One cannot underestimate the influence Charivari and the proprietors, the Weisers, had on the fashion landscape in New York City in the 1980s. The pantheon of visionary New York retailing families like the Weisers, the Pressmans, the Grodds, the Fortunoffs, and the Modells (among others) represented family retailing dynasties that changed the face of fashion and retail and made an indelible imprint in New York fashion and culture. Selma Weiser was indeed one of the last grandes dames of the retail business and her keen eye, vision, and style far exceeded the size and number of her stores. A portly redheaded dynamo, Selma was one of the pioneers on the Upper West Side and told me that as a young divorcée with two young children, she opened a boutique on the West Side when no one ventured there, and she hired live go-go dancers in the window to drive traffic.

The Weisers soon signed us up, as we were flush with our success with Kenneth Cole. My campaign tagline for Charivari, "Expect the unexpected," soon became associated with this influential brand and its consumers. One of the great things that made Charivari successful was that you never knew what great new thing you were going to discover in one of its stores. They had cutting-edge inventory and we created a campaign around that fact alone: *on the edge*. It is so sad today how the shopping experience has become so segregated and banal,

Reaching the pinnacle of fashion

but there was always an element of fashion frisson and of surprise when you flipped through the racks of Charivari. That *was* Charivari. Truly *the unexpected*. And we blanketed New York with the unique black-and-white photography campaign. This element of surprise and wow factor led us to a creative strategy we used throughout our campaigns.

Jon and Barbara, Selma's children who grew up in the business, were visionaries in their own way. They discovered and presented Japanese designers to the United States and New York and were the first to bring Yohji Yamamoto to America. At one particular shoot, a youthful fit of enthusiasm and passion got the better of me, and I actually got into a fistfight with the arrogant (but talented) fashion photographer who wouldn't take direction. I dodged taxis in the middle of Fifty-seventh Street, and we exchanged punches. For my efforts, Jon and Barbara pressed a Yohji blazer (with shark-tooth buttons and silk ribbons) into my hot little hands as a reward, and suddenly I was walking New York in Yohji jeans and a Yohji blazer, and my trademark green lizard cowboy boots. (Hence, my look in the *New York Magazine* photo for the "Ad Brats" article.) Jon Weiser actually advised me to take the blazer and jeans, put them in my closet, and look at them every few years as a time capsule of eighties' fashion. I do this on occasion to a wistful response.

RULE OF ENGAGEMENT

Perhaps I remain wistful over the entire Yohji episode because it reminds me of the critical foundation for running a successful business: having passion. As my friend Ed McMahon once told me, "You have to love your clients' products." Clients can feel either your passion or disinterest, and you can't fake it. I've taken this romantic notion one step further. In many ways, accounts and agencies often develop all the characteristics of a love relationship. There's the "getting to know you" dating phase (the account review), the "engagement phase" (the awarding of the account over other agencies), the "honeymoon phase" (the agency and client reveling and basking in the glow of their choice), the "marriage phase" (creating the contract, the planning of the work, and the research), and the "baby phase" (producing the work and the results).

Two remaining outcomes are possible.

Either you settle into a long-term, happy marriage (navigating the bumps in the road), or you stay married for a certain amount of time and then separate or divorce. If a separation does occur and the client decides to start dating again (play the field), the agency might be invited to "participate in the review process." Or the client might just initiate a divorce. Keeping a client in a long-term happy marriage takes time, work, commitment, and love—just like the regular institution. In any successful service business, there is a difference between getting the occasional project from a client and having a long-term, sustainable account relationship in which to build your business. These accounts are prized, not only because they are hard to get but because they give an agency scale, revenue, or both. One could almost look upon them as building blocks for an agency. And in the best circumstances, both the accounts and the agencies can become associated with each other. Industry examples have been Pepsi and BBDO, Nike and Wieden + Kennedy, and Burger King and Crispin Porter + Bogusky.

Hopefully, the accounts allow the agency to do work that yields both fame and fortune for the client, and fame and fortune for the agency. Interestingly, agencies and clients also develop reputations much like people do. If an agency is married for too many years and the work becomes "stale," it can develop a reputation for being big and boring, and it might end in cheating or divorce. If an agency loses too many accounts, it can develop a reputation for being "flighty" and/or in "a downward spiral." Most clients can also develop reputations, although they are sometimes unaware or too arrogant to believe it. They can become a "notorious player" if they date too many agencies in too many years and/or a get a "deadbeat dad" reputation if they stiff agencies on their fee or don't pay their bills. The worst reputation of all is if they steal an agency's ideas or people and don't pay for it. Only the most desperate of agencies will deal with clients who have the audacity to behave like this.

Agencies and clients also develop a seven-year itch. We've had many clients for exactly seven years (whether we resigned the business or vice versa): Kenneth Cole (which we resigned for Coach), Snapple, and Target to name a few. A few of our longest standing relationships have been with Schieffelin & Somerset, where we handled Hennessy and Moët & Chandon for more than sixteen years.

When today corporate M&A investment bankers buy brands, they all want a three-to-five-year return on investment. This dictates agency changes in dizzying speed, which our ad biz predecessors never anticipated. This has spawned what I call the eighteen-month chief marketing officer. When I first got into the business, a CMO held a long-term, valued position. My dear friend Clint Rodenberg was an esteemed CMO, and we worked together for almost twenty years. Today, CMOs come and go by default of the owner and the economy. The same happens to agencies. I believe all these changes actually make long-term clients more valuable, and I believe they need to be appreciated even more.

Many years ago, the agency was awarded the hotly contested Kao business. Kao is a Japanese-based company that owns such prestigious brands as Jergens, John Frieda, Curél, Bioré, and Ban deodorant. The entire account was up for review. I'll never forget getting the call from the president/CEO, Bill Gentner, who gave us the nod. I couldn't have been happier and promised Bill I would always look after the account personally, which I believe I have delivered on. If you looked up "great advertising client" in the dictionary, Bill's face would appear. He is thoughtful, visionary, fair, and supportive of the agency and doing great work over the years. We've had many successes (one or two misfires) but have created a great deal of great work together.

One great success we worked together on was a pioneer product called Jergens Natural Glow. The product is a lotion that had tanning benefits, but it looks and feels like a department store brand that's sold at mass price point. This high-quality product at a lower price point helped to propel this sub-brand to huge success, second only to the Jergens base brand. It was featured in the Style section of the *Times,* and people went crazy for it, spiking the demand. Sometimes when something is initially sold out or hard to get, it creates more of a feeding frenzy, and Natural Glow was a hit. This high/low strategy both surprises and delights consumers when they think they are, in fact, having "reverse sticker shock" because they think they are finding a department store product at a mass CVS kind of price.

I have always felt strongly that while women want gorgeous tans and glowing legs, arms, and décolletage, they also want their faces to glow as well. If you'd ever seen the movie *The Flamingo Kid,* it takes place in a beach club not to dissimilar too the one I used to belong to growing up (Westbury in Atlantic Beach). Although I was there in the seventies and eighties (not the fifties), not that much has changed. I still remember the wooden lockers, cabanas, mah-jongg, and snack bar. I also remember all the women lined up on their lounge chairs tanning (like Grandma Elsie and her sisters) and really giving their skin a good "shake and bake" with high-octane, powder-blue, tinfoil-lined reflectors. This memory prompted me to discuss an idea I had with Bill. One night at dinner, I said, "Bill, women don't just want their glow to stop here (I pointed at my neck), but all over. Even though Jergens and Natural Glow were yet to go into the face arena, Bill quickly agreed and Natural Glow Face was on the shelves before you could say "George Hamilton."

The high/low strategy we used for Natural Glow we also used for another Kao company, John Frieda. John Frieda makes incredible and innovative hair products, and they lead in inventiveness, effectiveness, and style. John Frieda, himself, started as a salon owner and developed breakthrough products that remain a core of their business today, like Frizz-Ease serum (which some have called the penicillin of hair). Having had many crucial strategic discussions over time, there was a change in chief marketing officers, and when I met the new one, David Stern, he asked me what I thought the biggest issue (at the time) for the brand was. I said, we, the client, and the agency had to identify and commit to the question, "Are we a mass/class brand? Or a class-for-mass brand?" The distinction may be hard to see at first blush, but the brand will act differently by choosing either path.

A mass/class brand like Natural Glow tries to appeal first and foremost to the widest audience by delivering the best available highest-end products. While class-for-mass brands target the upper end of the mass market and try to speak more to the top of the pyramid of their true consumers, rather than appealing to a biggest common denominator. To David's credit, he, first and foremost, was able to come back to the agency with an actual decision (which is rare!). Secondly, the decision was that John Frieda was a class-for-mass brand, appealing to the style leaders at mass and invoking their European styling heritage, i.e., London and Paris. This strategic decision was able to give the packaging and marketing a higher-end, chicer, and edgier image. I saluted David and Frieda for their clarity and by the year's end sales increased and continue to.

That level of trust, mutual respect, and action don't often happen in the halls of corporate America. When great clients partner with their agencies and great product development partners with marketing (and the handcuffs are taken off), great things can happen. Clients want to see passion from their agency. They want proactive ideas and a constant flow of talent. I, for one, roam the aisles of Duane Reade at night looking to see "the wall"; how the Kao products are faced and stocked and, of course, what the competition is up to. Store checks are important, and not everybody does it. What new product is your competitor hawking? What promotion and giveaway is shrink-wrapped?

I also believe in trying all the products even if they're for women! I'm not sure what my cleaning lady must think, but if you open my medicine cabinet you'll see antiaging eye products, skin cream, and volumizing hair products. I also think, as in every relationship, you have to take time to rekindle the spark and the love. We often create Ten Big Idea programs for our clients that offer them Ten Big Ideas gratis, or we will plan an all day off-site to brainstorm about new ideas for the brand. This is the equivalent to Mom and Dad going on a quickie romantic weekend and reaffirming their love.

With all my clients, it has been easy to see you can't fake passion, and I live on both sides of the fence; the adman and the consumer. Part of having a passion for a category is the external ad part of it as well as the internal—this intuitive combination of the head (like the Charivari line) and the heart. This ability to not only to digest research, but find the inherent trends, which can unlock a brand.

GETTING HIGH ABOUT HIGH/LOW

Almost a decade later, 1996, the seminal roles of personal passion and creativity in trendsetting were still (and always will be) a clarion call for me for successful branding. I was watching the Oscar telecast in the living room of my Ninth Street apartment. And while usually banal and vanilla, I saw something incredible and, to this day, I am not sure if the person involved has truly received proper credit in pop culture. Sharon Stone walked out on the red carpet and stage looking stunning in a Gap T-shirt and a Valentino skirt. While I have never met Sharon Stone, she is clearly a fashion icon and from what I have read, a Mensa. From that moment on, her fashion choice created a trend that (in my mind) has relaunched the way the American public thinks about style. Sharon Stone's bold fashion statement (like my Kirshenbaum designer jeans at Syracuse) said, "I am not going to be dictated to. I have a mind of my own, and I can mix and match, high and low, as I see fit." And this was America's first mass high/low *fashion* moment. Not to mention a bright star's decision to shine on her own by going against the Hollywood designer Mafia. Sharon not only expressed her own particular POV (go, girl), but in my opinion made a statement that would cause a seismic shift in what people wore and *how* they wore it. We had successfully been using this high/low strategy in cosmetics and hair care, and in my opinion, our campaigns for these accounts were somewhat trendsetting (walk down any pharmacy aisle, and you'll see what I mean). This trend in the ether would reinforce the way we saw the look for Target and the resulting, soon-to-be-famous fashion housewares campaign. For instance, we used a highbrow fashion image by mixing and using such mundane low-cost items as a sweater and lampshade, which we used as a skirt. We used a carburetor ring as an Elizabethan neck ruffle, shot on an iconic redhead. The juxtaposition of high image and low price point changed the retail landscape and paved the way for other zeitgeist brands, like H&M.

Sharon Stone's statement was also a testament to the power of authentic, personal creativity. Unlike sports teams where the sum is greater then the parts, there's a great deal of ego in the creative process; there's playing at it, and there's *being* it. Creative people want to shine, and I have found running creative departments that they don't necessarily want to share their ideas in groups or do what everyone else is doing. They want to stand out and do it on their own. And who can blame them?

Weirdly, being creatively independent is the exact opposite of what most American organized groups—sports teams, the military, sororities, fraternities (and yes, I was in one)—teach you to be. They encourage the group dynamic above the individual, and most people buy into it because that's what they've been taught from a young age. It's hard to stand alone when a group dynamic is also the social norm. It also doesn't encourage individuality, much less creativity.

Times have changed from when I was a kid, though, and individuality from a young age no longer equates to being an oddball like it did when everyone was watching *Wonderama*. Many men now confide that they wish they were creative or had gone into the advertising business, and many of the macho Penn or Notre Dame alums I know now send me their kids for internships. Many of their kids are now in film or theater schools as well. It's suddenly become acceptable to breed creative kids.

When I tell adult men that when I was nine years old I actually got kicked *off* Little League for not being good enough, they tend to look at me with a blank stare and are at a loss for words. Not that I really minded (except for the principle of it). After all, I wasn't a kid who really wanted to be hanging out all day in the hot sun in center field. I really did ask my father if I could bring out a folding chair to *sit* center field!

It is not untrue that two macho parent coaches got together and said, "We're never gonna win with that Kirshenbaum kid, you know the *creative* one," and that I was summarily given the boot and dispatched to a ragtag, loser team somewhere in Rockville Centre. My writing skills at nine were in full force when I wrote a soliloquy to the coaches and cc'd the regional Little League office. And although everyone was very contrite when I accused them of *not* fostering sportsmanship, I rather lost my taste for team sports. Hurt at the time, I became more creatively defiant and aloof. I can't say I'm sorry about the experience now, although I cannot really believe (being a parent) that two grown men would actually do that to a young kid. At any rate, it did teach me that creativity does often mean standing out from the pack. And I'm not a big believer in *team creativity*. It is rarely productive. Coming up with creative ideas really does mean thinking against the grain, being a contrarian, and going up against the odds.

A few years back, I was invited to participate in a group creative SWAT team to help one of the country's most prominent senators on his presidential bid for office. High-level creative directors and industry notables were invited to a conference room in midtown to meet the senator and to brainstorm ideas. I decided to go, but immediately knew it was a disaster after five minutes.

The first half of the meeting just had people introducing themselves and puffing out their chests at their own credentials. The candidate then went on to drone for an hour and a half without asking anyone's opinion. We were then told to do a group brainstorm after which he would choose his favorite campaign theme. I immediately knew that the candidate would never win, let alone get nominated. Unlike Margaret Thatcher who'd hired the Saatchi brothers in London in 1979 (and gave them the creative freedom to do their thing), this candidate and his people didn't understand the creative process and thought a group creative *gang bang* would get the best results. Well, they wouldn't even be able to order lunch with that thinking.

After listening to windbags pontificate for two hours, I suggested the senator's long speeches might be too long-winded and that people might want to have a dialogue with him instead of having him talk at them. The candidate and his folk looked at me like I had three heads. That suited me just fine because I wasn't going to work in a group with pompous, annoying ad people anyway. You can't get to creative genius without honesty, and you can't get *there* in a team with lowest common denominator thinking. Regardless of your political opinion of Obama, he and his team understood modern marketing dialogue and social media, and that's one of the reasons why *he's* in office. I promptly told the senator's team I was too busy. As with Little League, I'm not into team sports. Especially creative ones.

To be truly creative, you have to have confidence and fortitude to know you are right even when everyone is telling you you're wrong. And most importantly you have to be able to have the confidence to give your clients the right advice and not tell them only what they want to hear. My proudest moments have often been my most difficult ones, where I've come up against strong personalities and people who are so successful you need to reach into your inner core to defend your point of view. Unlike the senator and his team, successful people who actually take advice and *then* make their own decisions usually are the ones who are most successful.

In 2002, I received a wonderful call from Steve Wynn who asked me to be in Vegas on Monday. It was Friday. I, of course, jumped on a flight and met Steve and his wife, Elaine, who I remember being incredibly elegant in Chanel as she gave me a tour of their facilities in a golf cart. After all of his incredible successes and the remarkable Bellagio, among others, he was branding a different kind of hotel and hired us to assist him. I say (respectfully) assist because one doesn't much go it alone when it comes to working with Steve and Elaine.

Look up the word *perfectionist* in the dictionary, and you'll see the Wynns. Steve and Elaine had been the best by carefully supervising *every* detail—and I mean *every* detail from the carpets and finish on the drapery fabric to the naming and logos of the properties. They even made a model of the new casino on their property to see it in 3-D. And they hired the best people. The best designers. The best chefs. The best of everything. Steve also knows the names of all his employees. I was so impressed when he took me through a casino tour and said hello to a random croupier. "Hi, Sid," Steve said, "how's that nice family of yours?" "Fine, Steve," the croupier said, and waved. Originally, Steve wanted to name the new hotel and casino after his prized Picasso, *Le Rêve*. Having spent much of my career in naming, I have always believed the American market likes names that are easy to pronounce, and *Le Rêve* could be pronounced two ways: Le Reeve or Le Reve. I also felt that while *Le Rêve* was one of Picasso's most famous paintings, the idea was a bit obscure.

Now I'm sure Steve has heard for years that his name is the best name in gaming. Certainly because he's the King of Vegas, but also because of the double entendre. Who wouldn't want to have a name homophonous with winning? It goes without saying that after a lot of thinking, clearly I thought naming the new casino Wynn was the best idea. I know Steve had been thinking about calling his new creation The Wynn, and I am not taking credit for it, but sometimes you need a *no*-man, not a *yes*-man to bounce ideas off of. I found an obscure book that had taken Judy Garland's personal signature and then the type designer did a lovely professional polish on it. And that's what I proposed for Steve. Steve bought off on the logo idea, which would be a refined version of his very own signature, and we created the logo and business card and stationery. For all his supposed "sight" issues, I sat with Steve for more than two hours as he personally went through each and every business card when the stock came in and he picked out the three or four (from hundreds) that were off-register for color—and he was right!

I really enjoyed working with Steve and Elaine and thought they were visionary, gracious, lovely, and professional. My only issue was the trip to and from Vegas. My twins (I have three children) had just been born, and I didn't like being away from home. While I can't boast a long relationship with Steve, I do think his lovely signature adds a nice touch to the Vegas skyline.

In my humble opinion, if you're not prepared to have a real opinion and to go against the tide, you'll never ever ride the wave to fame and fortune. Whether you take a look at the King of Vegas or the Queen of the Red Carpet, Steve and Sharon didn't get to where they are by running with the pack. Passion, vision and, most importantly, an intelligent individuality have helped both achieve incredible fame through breaking the mold. That's just as true for advertising as it is for individuals.

CHAPTER EIGHT
AD LAND, THE PLACE WHERE ART MEETS COMMERCE

ADMEN CLEARLY NEED TO HAVE an artistic vision as an integral part of their creativity. And if they are able to tap into or embrace that vision, so much the better. Given that, it's no surprise that admen have always been great art collectors. Since advertising is one of the few businesses where art meets commerce, it's only natural. After all, who would have a better-trained eye for the emerging new or the remarketing of the old, then an adman? Art and the art world are (hopefully) in our ad DNA. Just this year, the daughter of a legendary adman sold her Picasso for a record price. From Jay Chiat to Charles Saatchi's own personal London museum, The Saatchi Gallery, admen lead the way with great vision, innovation, collections, and sponsorship in the art world.

A few years ago, one of Dana's closest friends, Andrea, married Marc Glimcher, the scion of the Pace Gallery. Not only did Marc become one of my closest friends but, as chance and luck would have it, he also became my art adviser/art dealer as well. He helped broaden my interest in abstract and conceptual art, and we actually made news together in the *New York Times* when one of his artists, Keith Tyson, became the first artist to actually turn a sculpture into a billboard. Keith's idea was to create the first sculpture that actually "rented" itself out as a billboard. It was in the shape of a cube on which we ran ads for our client John Frieda Hair Care. They paid for it and voilà—the *first* billboard sculpture was born.

Besides having a pretty picture on the wall or as sculpture on the coffee table, art also inspires. Where we derive inspiration from can vary, but unless you feed your creative soul on a regular basis, the output can become limited or stale. The round bold circles of my Calder gouache *Red Sea* helped give me a sense of confidence when it came to using the Target bull's-eye solo within the Target advertising. Traveling to Europe and appreciating classic French Impressionist art and vintage poster art helped me to design the Hennessy Martini posters. We launched the martini as a "rediscovered" cocktail from the 1920s. Most bars do not allow or want advertising, but our classic Hennessey Martini poster art was embraced and hung in upscale bars and restaurants. It was truly framed advertising masquerading as art! Typography, design, fashion, architecture, and style all go into making relevant and gorgeous advertising as well as marketing. And unless you believe there's an art to creating an ad and selling it to begin with, it won't turn out very artful.

Sometimes you need to treat the advertising medium *as* art as well. For Snapple, we created an actual Snapple typeface that was both whimsical and quirky, and represented the brand, as there wasn't a typeface in the marketplace that was, in our opinion, *Snapple-like*. For our Judith Leiber charity event for ACRIA (we sponsor at least one pro bono event each year), our PR and promo unit LIME secured well-known artists to design a Judith Leiber bag. Eric Fischl and Ross Bleckner, among others, created the most gorgeous one-of-a-kind pieces of jeweled art bags that were auctioned off for the great cause. For Stolichnaya, I asked Diane von Furstenberg to design a signature Diane/Stoli print that graced a fashion

Shoptalk
By Tim Nudd

Advertising That Sure Is Art
Richard Kirshenbaum places ads on Keith Tyson work

Talk about media-neutral: Kao Brands has paid an undisclosed fee to appear on four sides of a cube-shaped sculpture by **Keith Tyson**, a British artist whose 45-piece exhibition titled "Geno Pheno" has been showing at the Pace Wildenstein gallery in Manhattan's Chelsea district for about a week.

The ads were placed by **Richard Kirshenbaum**, a longtime art collector and co-chairman of Kao ad agency Kirshenbaum Bond + Partners, at the request of the gallery.

"My job is to make sure they're front and center with popular culture ... and having your brand show up in a museum or an art gallery is not exactly a bad thing," says Kirshenbaum. The idea behind the piece, called *Chameleon*, was to create a work of art that reflects society's changes through advertising, says **Andrea Glimcher**, director of communications for the gallery. When Kao's year-long contract is up, the company will have an opportunity to renew or pass along the space to another advertiser, Glimcher says.

It may not be the kind of return on investment that art collectors are usually looking for, but considering the gallery's asking price—$85,000, according to sources—the anonymous buyer may be looking for any and all cash-back incentives. Glimcher would not disclose how much the buyer paid. Tyson won England's prestigious Turner Prize in 2002. If marketers know him at all, it might be for a piece he did several years ago in which he cast the entire contents of a Kentucky Fried Chicken menu in lead.

The first ad sculpture

show as a signature fabric for dresses and even as wrapping paper for the holidays. We inserted it into magazines for consumers to use for their holiday wrap. For Timex, LIME approached legendary designers like Karim Rashid to design artful new Timex pieces. Since the watches were so cool, we even helped Timex get alternate distribution in hot stores, like the retailer Scoop, to introduce the new artful Timex watches.

However, in order to be artful, one needs to understand art.

So if you're just starting out and don't know that much about art, look everywhere. Read magazines about art and artists. One of the best ways to see what's really going on is to get out and visit the galleries in major cities. Another way to really see and experience art is to go to museums or follow the auction houses such as Sotheby's or Christie's, which, in my opinion, is a better use of time than any museum because you get to see how much the art is actually worth. I have taken to calling the auction houses museums with prices!

Quite frankly, advertising is a mirror of society, and art is the actual reflection. Art, design, architecture, and fashion are all linked. For example, in the 1940s, most wealthy Americans aped Paris fashion and decor. And if you lived in an apartment on Fifth or Park Avenue, it was most likely filled with imported boiserie and Louis XV–style furniture. Since that was the style of the day, they most likely wanted a sedate and beautiful Renoir or Monet above the sofa because it went with the decor. Just look at glamorous movies of the era, and you'll see French decor or French art show up in the set design.

Today, there has been an explosion in contemporary and mid-century art prices because today's young Wall Street tycoons want contemporary apartments, with contemporary furniture and contemporary art over the sofa. The hedgie wife wants a Louis Vuitton Murakami bag. And whether it's a 1950s' Josef Albers's *Homage to the Square,* a Rothko, a Koons, a Warhol *Campbell's Soup Can,* or a Damien Hirst, it's all interlinked and intertwined. The sedate rosy-cheeked girl in a bonnet by Renoir may not look as cool (to some people) over a sleek Italian sofa! But that said, there is always a strong market for the best art regardless of its era—and how it might look over the sofa. Design influences art, and advertising influences and reflects both! It's all integrated, and all influential. In order to be on the cutting edge visually, you need to feel the pulse and be in the know for your clients.

I once took a friend to hear Arthur Miller speak not too long before he passed. It was an evening at The Lotos Club, which is a wonderful literary club in New York that was founded by Mark Twain. I am proud to be a member and was excited to see and meet the man who wrote *Death of a Salesman*, but who also was married to Marilyn Monroe (and she converted—how hot is that?). Before he closed his speech, he looked out at the intimate audience and said, "I am always asked why art is so important. If you go to any museum in the world and study ancient civilizations, you won't see or hear about the bankers or the shoe manufacturers. What is left, after all is said and done, is the art."

Arthur Miller was presumably referring to visual art: painting, sculpture, jewelry, pottery, etc. But his own art form, the written word, is just as important.

*　　*　　*　　*

Regardless of the inspiration, the written word has always intrigued me, whether by poem, book, or song. Joni Mitchell's early album, *Blue,* had a huge impact on me as a young teen. And her lyrics still do. The idea that in this day and age one can still earn a living or make a true impact by the turn of a phrase or a clever thought was and is provocative, if not downright sexy. I still marvel at getting paid for copywriting or naming services, as if there is something illicit and unreal about earning your living from words and thoughts in a more mercenary world.

Of course, when you're an adman, you never know just who the client will be and how involved they are with the written word. Like the time we met with the Rolling Stones. I did get a particular thrill when a manufacturing group asked us to come up with a campaign to sell a Rolling Stones clothing line. Our creative team at the time, Bill Oberlander, David Buckingham, and I, brainstormed a fairly provocative campaign using the tongue and the words "Open Wide." Not exactly demure but hey, neither is "Sticky Fingers." We all flew off to Detroit to see and present to the Stones. After partying and actually getting thrown out of the stadium by security in true rocker fashion, we went back to the hotel to prepare for our meeting. Some member of the entourage basically said I was the one to present to the band because I had long hair and was astute enough to wear a black leather motorcycle jacket. I remembered it was sort of surreal presenting to Mick (those lips) and Keith and the crew. They were enthusiastic and polite enough but, in true fashion, we were probably, in hindsight, being used as part of some pitch to the Stones and the project never went anywhere. That said, I still have my black leather jacket with the Rolling Stones Steel Wheels Backstage Pass VIP sticker on it (which is now probably memorabilia worth money), and we got a great concert out of it. But talk about copy or lyrics—one tough audience!

Regardless of the manner in which an ad's words are conveyed, an ad can sometimes wield power as opposed to just being commercially successful or artistic. I was especially proud when Robert Kennedy Jr. hired the agency for his environmental group, Riverkeeper, and actu-

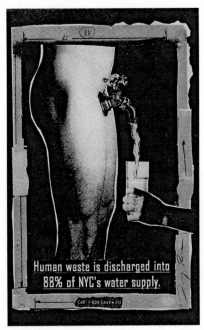

Appetizing! Right?
No wonder it worked!

ally used our provocative pro bono campaign as leverage and to advance his green agenda. One ad was a photo of toothpaste on a toilet brush with the headline "10,780,000 gallons of sewage are discharged into NYC's water supply each day." Another ad had a faucet in the place of a man's penis talking about waste going into the water supply. Our brave copywriter, Josh Miller, dropped trou for that one! Kennedy took the campaign to persuade then-mayor David Dinkins to crack down on environmental regulations and help buy land around the reservoirs to protect the water at the source as opposed to having to treat it. If he would not do so, we would run the outrageous campaign.

Dinkins took one look at the campaign and agreed to support Kennedy's plan (since it was an election year). Since it was such a successful "conversation," that campaign never actually ran, giving it the distinction of "the most effective ads that never ran." That said, we made a commitment to do at least one public service campaign a year and have worked with many fine not-for-profits over the years, and I'm proud of our public service record.

Ads can be pretty, striking, provocative, breakthrough, disturbing, or even sexy. They all bear the relationship to the environment we live in. If well crafted, they can inspire, like art. If well crafted, they can inspire, like art. These days, they even appear in museums. Ads have started to migrate from being just a commercial effort to pop culture. Did anyone say soup can?

THE CAMPAIGN

CHAPTER NINE
GO WEST, YOUNG MAN

AH, THE WEST COAST. The sun, the stars, the palm trees.

Oh, did I mention the traffic, the smog, and the fact that nobody walks? For me, LA is one of those places that are perfect when you're young, good-looking, and single. Or old, ugly, and rich.

I did have a complete love affair with LA from the early days of the agency, not only because I went on regular five-star shoots but because I was in the young and single stage, not to mention that there were exciting meetings to be had with movie studios that were looking for a new creative resource and agency shoots as well. And presumably, they hoped we were bringing passion and vision to the mix.

Given my hotel proclivities, I'd become a habitué of the Beverly Hills Hotel. I thought there was something very "vacationy" about spending time at the pool before and after a meeting, and the Beverly Hills Coffee Shop is still my favorite restaurant in LA. To this day, people could give me the best table at LA's newest, hippest restaurant, and I'd rather take a pass and mosey on over to the swivel bar stools in the coffee shop for a vanilla egg cream. It has the best grilled burgers and tuna or chicken salad sandwiches, all freshly prepared right in front of you by women (probably named Dolores) in pink-and-white starched uniforms behind the fifties' kidney-shaped bar. Aged Hollywood stars sit there pondering their careers over a perfectly cooked grilled cheese. As my life always seems defined by eating, business meetings were punctuated by first having a meal at the coffee shop (as discussed they make a *sick* egg cream) or inviting a prospective client to have a Cobb salad at the pool (chopped, hold the ham, blue cheese on the side) with crispy french fries (perfection).

In those early days, we secured projects from Dino De Laurentiis and Fox, among others. It's not just fiction that studio executives really do communicate in LA "marketing speak," and projects are always briefed in vague yet illustrative descriptions. For example, a fresh-faced twenty-something studio exec would gesticulate, "We need a campaign for this new show. It's like *Jurassic Park* meets *The Simpsons*, etc." My favorite was one studio executive's description of a billboard assignment we did for the soon to be launched *21 Jump Street*, starring the newcomer Johnny Depp. "All you need to know," the producer said with the corresponding hand motion, is "think girls, guys, and guns." This intellectual briefing produced a billboard and a creative campaign for this highly anticipated show, and we plastered Johnny above Sunset Boulevard, a baby-faced, soon-to-be star waving a big ole Colt 45.

Being young and single, I did manage to date one or two Hollywood girls (neurotic New Yorkers who became executives). I never had a thing for actresses (too self-centered) or models (too vacant), and I also managed to rebuff the advances of quite a few Hollywood executives who wanted me to walk on the other side of the street, but it appeared to me that having a relationship with someone in LA was transitory, and I preferred the girls back home. My friends, however, were constantly moving either from from New York to LA or to New York from LA, and I spent quite a lot of time at the BHH or in Malibu where everyone seemed to have a hot tub and a eucalyptus tree. There was something glam about shooting Helena Christensen on a beach in Malibu with legendary photographer Herb Ritts for the launch of Diesel. He ordered the supermodel and her buff male cohort to roll around in the surf and sand in their Diesel jeans with complex directions like "Work it!" and "Come on, I want to see some tongue!" After the shoot wrapped, I did learn one of *my* greatest lessons about women. When Helena stripped down to her panties for a wardrobe fitting in one of the BHH bungalows, I asked this gorgeous creature what perfume she was wearing, as I found it intoxicating. Perhaps I found the semi-naked sight of her intoxicating, but I promptly bought Dana (then my new girlfriend) a bottle of it as a souvenir from the shoot. I really did think I was being so *thoughtful*! At first, I couldn't understand why Dana promptly threw the bottle in the garbage, only later understanding that no woman wants her boyfriend to be reminded of a semi-naked supermodel who he was ogling at in a Beverly Hills Hotel bungalow!

Semi-naked models (and mannequins) confronting me all the time. Not totally nude ones!

As much as I like LA, it always felt very much like aerated cotton candy—sweet to the taste, but no substance. Until, of course, Ed McMahon called and we opened up our LA office in his house! One of the great things about kbp was you never knew who was going to call and walk through the door. Everyone was welcome, and the more ridiculous the situation the better. It seemed that Ed and his newish, great wife, Pam, were friendly with the Lutzes from General Motors. They had heard about us, and Pam and Denise were friends and wanted to earn some extra cash by recommending new business. It was an immediate opportunity and voilà—we opened our very own West Coast service office in Ed's house. As I recall, we paid Pam and Denise a modest draw against commissions. And within days, Ed was answering the phone in his Beverly Hills home, saying, "Heeere's Kirshenbaum and Bond Partners West."

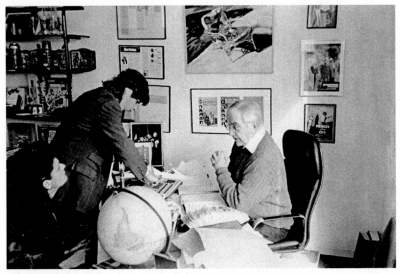

Heeere's Ed sitting at my desk

Ed was one of the great pitchmen of his day, and I learned a great deal from him. Regardless of what anybody could say, you also have to understand that Ed was Hollywood royalty and knew everyone and everyone knew him. Before he became ill, walking into a restaurant with Ed was like walking in with the president. Everyone said hello and wanted to shake his hand. That's because everyone had grown up with him on *The Tonight Show*, and who wouldn't love a guy who was known for delivering a check for a million dollars to your door! In all actuality, he was cooler than the coolest indie actor who didn't give a damn. "The peoples" loved Ed, and Ed loved "his peoples"! He also had the most colorful stories. He'd started out on the Atlantic City Boardwalk as a carnie and went to Hollywood to become an announcer. Now, there is something of a fact that some people are born with what we call a radio voice in the business. It is a golden-throated, mellifluous voice and, of course, Ed had it. With his trademark smile and twinkle in his eye, he could sell everything. And sell he did. Ed told me he made huge amounts of money in the days when people barely made anything. He knew he overspent and had too many homes, which can be more than a bit expensive. Ed told me at the height of his earning years he'd bought the Hollywood home of David O. Selznick and Irene Mayer (Louis B. Mayer's daughter). That's before Ed's wife ran off with the cop and all the bad investments.

Ed also taught me one of the great lessons in the advertising business. When I asked him how he got the gig to become the spokesperson for Anheuser-Busch, he relayed the following story: It seemed that before Ed they were considering an actor as a spokesperson who was involved in some sort of scandal. He was called into the corporate office to discuss the matter and when asked what he wanted to drink the actor promptly ordered a whiskey, or some such drink. Two days later, Ed was invited in to meet the senior Mr. Busch. When asked what *he* wanted to drink, Ed asked for a Bud. The previous actor was tossed and Ed got one of the most lucrative jobs in advertising because he ordered and liked the *client's product*. Ding! Ding! Ding! Ed also added that initially they were going to hire the actor but just give him a good talking-to, but when he wasn't smart enough to order an Anheuser-Busch product, they passed on him. Ed put his arm around me and said, "Rich, always order your client's products. They want to know you love it as much as they do. And if you don't want to, don't take the business!" This lesson has stood the test of time. And no one is more brand loyal than me. Except, perhaps, Brandpa.

While Jon and I have always followed this brand philosophy, we did make the same kind of mistake as the actor Ed spoke of did. It was in our first few years of business (well before we met Ed)! Cathie Black, who was running Hearst, had recommended us to the owners of *USA Today,* the Curley brothers. We'd prepared this great spec ad, which essentially was a full page taken from the *New York Times,* just a portion of which was highlighted in yellow marker. A headline read, "All the news that's fit to read," or something like that, signed off by *USA Today.* In the meeting, the Curley brothers looked squarely across the conference table and asked us if we read *USA Today* and/or had a subscription. In typical twenty-something logic, we answered, "No, and that's why you need us." The honesty didn't work with *les frères* Curley, and we were summarily given the boot. Needless to say, after the meeting I just went out and bought another pair of green lizard cowboy boots to console myself, which soon became something of a trademark.

*　　*　　*　　*

Having our office in Ed's house was not without its perks, like the time he and Pam invited me to Disney to be a judge on *Star Search* after I had lunch with them at the Disney replica of the Brown Derby restaurant. I remember sitting next to Marilyn McCoo or someone from the Fifth Dimension as we judged the children's competition. Ed established *American Idol* in his own way, lest we forget!

For Ed's sixty-ninth birthday (ahem), Pam threw this incredible party at their home and the theme was Ed's JAZZ joint. The Hollywood old guard was all there. Crazy people like Dick Clark, Freddie de Cordova, and Marvin and Barbara Davis (who was ablaze in all her diamonds). I wasn't married to Dana yet, but she came with me. We still laugh that when Ed introduced us to Marvin and Barbara, Dana kept looking at the floor. Finally, I asked her what she was looking for. After viewing Barbara's diamond ring (which was bigger than a skating rink), Dana shrugged and said, "Maybe a baguette or a diamond chip fell on the floor."

Ed taught me more than one thing I will never forget. He once told me that he lost a great deal of money in a business deal for an investor and paid back every cent *personally.* When we were out on the town, he was always gracious and stopped to give everyone a smile, a handshake, and a kind word. Old-school Hollywood has always appreciated their fan base, and no one was more elegant than Ed. He was the consummate gentleman. He reinforced the ideas that you loved and respected your fans and your clients, and that the public was made up of really good people who you should never, ever talk down to. Those have always been some of the primary tenets of kbp, in part because of Ed. Ed had something many people in Hollywood don't have. He had character, class, and integrity, and I loved him for it. Even though our foray into LA was fun but short-lived, we, like many Mad Men before us, decided to open another California office. Of all the crazy, cockamamy things we'd ever done, opening up a San Francisco office would turn out to be one of the craziest.

People rave about San Francisco, but I found the vibe at the time to be a bit tiresome and pretentious. Restaurants serve things like "wilted lettuce" and "emulsified balsamic over tepid beef." I thought it took itself way too seriously, and I knew from the beginning we were in for trouble when I found out that all of the four-star restaurants I saw in the wine country were off a highway. Also, why go somewhere where there's an ocean and you can't even swim? I still can't get over how much people *love* San Francisco. They rave about it night and day. I don't mean to be a San Francisco buzzkill, but it always felt like it was the *United States of Generica* to me. I've learned a great lesson after all these years: If you don't like going somewhere, it's a good reason not to go there, and an even better one not to make an investment, or foolishly open an office there. The West Coast is littered with New York agency–failed offices. In fact, everyone who has ever opened a real, fully staffed office on the West Coast—save TBWA\Chiat\Day and Deutsch—has failed. In both cases, they had solid independent leadership, but that didn't stop us from heeding the siren call of stupidity.

Two confluences made the idea of a San Francisco office appealing. In New York, we had a big financial client who wanted a service office out west and secondly, we saw a way to let our people grow by having an additional office on the left coast. Poor judgment prevailed as we let others scope out the real estate and leases. I should have listened to my little voice. When our then-CFO laid a 20 percent gain a year on the table, I could have told you then that the advertising business doesn't only go up in a straight line (what investment does? Ahem . . .), but for some reason and for one of the only times in my life, our eyes were not on the ball. Now *everything* goes under the microscope, and I never let anyone pressure me to do anything that doesn't feel right at the time. I think I was just interested in other things—clients, food, art, and getting laid (not necessarily in that order). Not to mention appearing in press-related agency PR!

In short order, we negotiated one of the worst real estate deals in advertising history in an up-and-coming part of town that never *got up* or *came.* Not only were there yearly escalations in the lease, but we spent a pricey sum creating a design euphoria. The kicker was that the New York office guaranteed the lease. Luckily, the business was profitable and growing, but the lack of our presence ended up hurting us and our creative reputation. The problem with running a business on the West Coast is that it takes an entire day to fly back to New York, and New York opens three hours later. When you factor in the time difference and lack of interest we found in San Francisco and vice versa, it was a recipe for disaster. At first, we liked to go, staying in the wine country occasionally on the weekends after meetings. Then we went sporadically, but with so much going on in New York, eventually we couldn't be there, as much as we tried.

At any rate, there are only two ways to make money in the marketing space, in my opinion. Either you keep your overhead and people costs low, or you grow something really big. (Being in the middle sucks!) Now to be fair, as the Internet bubble was *bubbling,* the San Francisco office with its talented team raked in quite a handful and seemed to be a good move despite the overhead costs. Once the Internet bubble burst and the San Francisco real estate market crashed, we essentially had the best-designed office in the worst part of town. We tried to rent it to a methadone clinic, and even *they* turned it down. We did try to appeal to the landlord to lower the rent, and they did accommodate us to a point. But they knew the New York office was on the hook, and we paid and paid and paid. Now, knowing you are spending millions of dollars on virtually empty space can be quite galling, but in true kbp tradition, we just hunkered down and got more accounts to foot the bill. All in all, it did teach us a great lesson. Fixed hard costs and grandiose dreams (and only looking at the positive) could possibly sink even the most shipshape vessel. Looking at the upside is always important, but being realistic about the downside, doing your due diligence, and trying to have a conservative approach are the keys to any successfully run enterprise. Interestingly, I recently turned down an investment not because the upside didn't look good but because when I really looked at what the cost would be if the shit hit the fan, I wrote it off the legal bills and never looked back. After all, I may have left my wallet in San Francisco, but I'm not about to do that again.

It *is* a common mistake though. The West Coast always beckons to New York ad people the way fool's gold did during the gold rush. It usually has something to do with one of the founders dating an LA starlet or wanting to play tennis outside during the month of February. The next thing you know, voilà, an office is born. For me, my time in San Francisco felt more like time in San Quentin.

MOVIE STARS, MILLIONAIRES, AND BILLIONAIRES

All that said, when I first got into the ad business, A-list celebrities avoided appearing in advertising like the plague. In fact, it was a dirty little secret that the really big stars would do a campaign for a few cold "mil" for "some" product in Asia, as long as no one saw it in the States. These days, however, everyone is now clamoring to star, write, and direct ad campaigns. Times have indeed changed.

Once the recession hit Hollywood, a good portion of it showed up on my doorstep. Agents started to call on a regular press basis to let me know great stars were suddenly available, when, of course, I knew they already were (since very few movies were in production). Producers, who only get paid when a project is actually filming, showed up in droves to let me know they were suddenly "branding experts." Some were clever enough to offer me value (i.e., a star, a song, or interest in a project for my clients), but the vast majority lectured me on their branding expertise and told me they wanted to compete with me for ad dollars or, in fact, confided that they were prepared to become actual ad agencies when they came for advice or help. This only reinforced my opinion that I was thrilled to have gone into the "lower radar" advertising business rather than having decamped for LA and the film business at a young age (and become truly moronic).

I have always said that advertising is a glamour business, but on the lowest rung of the glamour ladder. But that, too, is changing. Ever since *Mad Men* became a hit, everyone wants "in" on the skinny ties, dry martinis, and inner workings of how "campaigns get done." Everyone now fancies themselves a branding "mogul." It's sort of interesting that after all these years people have finally come around to my way of thinking. It is also true that smarter, relevant stars are exerting their social media influence and iconic status to get percentages of companies they're involved with. And the worlds of advertising and entertainment are melding yet again. Stars like Ashton Kutcher for Popchips and Sean "P. Diddy" Combs for Cîroc vodka are creating new entrepreneurial deals, which use their social media cred to great results. P.S. *Great for them!*

However, no matter *who's* doing the work, the one person who really should be credited with this *Hollyweird adquake* is Mike Ovitz. Over a decade ago, he rattled the ad industry when his entertainment agency, CAA, was hired to do creative work for Coca-Cola. I had lunch with Mike recently and told him the fear he created in ad industry circles when he took on that work. He smiled wryly, but after hearing him passionately tell the story about how he landed the business it was apparent that Coca-Cola hadn't hired CAA as much as they'd hired Mike Ovitz. With his smarts, energy, well-cut suits, intellectual glasses, and quick-on-the-trigger personality, he didn't come across as much as a slick Hollywood guy but as a consummate adman!

That said, Hollywood and Madison Avenue may be blurring the lines, but two constants in the Hollywood culture always seem to remain: stars and sex. People still love the "stars du jour," and from the Wheaties box on down, stars-of-the-moment do sell. And sex, of course, always sells, even to women. All the talk about wanting to be a "*real* woman" is essentially bullshit in my opinion. I see women in focus groups in Texas and Long Island who have more in common than you think by way of big hair and big opinions, who tell you they want the "*natural look*"—speaking with their lacquered coiffed 'dos and pulled faces. At the end of the day, no one *really* wants to look like the girl next door. Everyone wants to look like Megan Fox or the sexpot of the moment. Therefore it is inevitable that Hollywood and Madison Avenue will always be attached at the proverbial hip, with ad people having to deal with the vagaries of Hollywood for many campaigns and marketing plans.

As for the stars, celebrity shelf life can be lucrative for a special few but also is somewhat limited. I am quite open to seeing the famous and the once famous troop through my office (for good material) with their "sometimes" bad plastic surgery and entourages of hangers-on discussing deals. Everyone knows it's somewhat of a charade. That said, Betty White is an example of someone who triumphed through a Super Bowl spot for Doritos to become a national darling in her eighth decade. A TV spot relaunched her as a national treasure, which only goes to show advertising not only sells products, but also sells stars if they are handled in the proper way.

I remember a wonderful story concerning a star du jour who was hired by a cosmetics company for a signature fragrance. Sometime, as in this case, I feel like Leonard Zelig, the changeable character in Woody Allen's movie, because even though I'm still in my forties, I feel like I've had the good fortune to be in all these different places with different people from different decades. Such as the set of *Dynasty* (yes, I am not kidding). While I didn't get to see Alexis and Crystal in a Nolan Miller catfight, I did have the unique experience of naming and working on (and I kid you not) the Joan Collins signature fragrance. And while the experience wasn't so sweet smelling, let's be clear: It doesn't get better than that from a material POV, Kathy Griffin!

Before I give you the poop on this one, I have to tell you right off the bat that Joan Collins is really gorgeous, and when she made her comeback on *Dynasty,* she was molten hot. She'd been hired by a small cosmetics company called Parlux (which was our client), and they debriefed me by letting me know that Joan had agreed to do a fragrance for them called Joan Collins' Hollywood. Yours truly took this at face value and created a campaign (even though I thought the name had a cheese factor and was somewhat perplexed that she had agreed to the name) and flew out to Hollywood to do a meet-and-greet with the great Madame Joan. I got in the white disco limo provided by someone to take me to the set of *Dynasty*. (If anything is more eighties than this, please let me know because I cannot top this and I was still orange and Ban de Soleil-ed from the pool and eating a Cobb salad. Well, maybe I can top it, since I appeared in an eighties' Joan Jett video with Sylvia Miles called *Good Music*, which is now on YouTube as a VH1 Classic!) I was also impressed by Sylvia's star quality when she marched into the room and demanded someone offer her a seat, stating "I want a seat, I was nominated for an Academy Award for *Midnight Cowboy*," as she delved into her pocketbook and fished out a sandwich.

No sooner did I meet in Collins's dressing room, then did she vomit all over the name of the fragrance. Not having named it, I promised I would have something for her in short order, went back to the hotel, and got ready for my flight home (though, not before having a BHH chicken salad sandwich on grilled toast and a vanilla egg cream with crispy fries). I do remember sitting at the coffee shop next to a famous television host, catatonic over a tuna melt, crying into his coffee since he'd aged out of his contract. But young Hollywood had not yet taken over and Cyd Charisse, Tony Martin, and a cast of glam characters played cards by the pool each and every day, giving the hotel a very Vegas feel. I was sorry to leave, especially at seeing Cyd Charisse's legendary legs in high heels by the cabanas and, of course, Sven, the famous pool boy.

On my time off, I happened to buy a fifties' lamp in an antique store on Melrose and when I flew back to New York, they wouldn't let me board the plane with it. And this was before 9/11 security! According to security, the lamp was in the shape of a gun (if you pulled the trigger, the light went on). I fought them, saying it was a lamp. I must say it was one of the few times in my life where I was almost arrested when I pointed the lamp at airport security, trying to show them the lightbulb. But security insisted it was a gun, and I could hold up the plane with a lamp, if I chose to, so they confiscated it and made me take my seat (next to Richard Gere) who, like everyone else in first class either thought I was a deranged decorator or a terrorist. I still pine for that lamp! Imagine a gun lamp! You pull the trigger and the lamp goes on. Genius. It's right up there with my lunch box collection that I installed in my office and then in the agency conference room for what I call *personality on a budget.*

The following month, I returned to LA to present the new name and the campaign to La Collins. This time, the meeting took place in her home above the Hollywood Hills. The house, which had been formerly owned by my friend's mother (the late comedienne Totie Fields) had, I kid you not, a gold Rolls-Royce parked on the white marble driveway. I recall the houseboy answering the door in his blue silk hot pants (but I cannot be certain).

However, I am certain that Joan had one of those great needlepoint pillows you see in tony Madison Avenue shops that read, "It's not the men in my life. It's the life in my men." How much better can you get than that? I was ushered in, and Nolan Miller was fitting her for a wig, but I do remember thinking that Joan Collins had one of the most beautiful architectural faces I had ever seen. Her eyes were widely set, and her cheekbones were incredible, and she stroked my arm in a harmless fashion proving she liked cashmere. Clearly, I was not her type, but she did lead the entire party through her bedroom (a mattress atop a pyramid) into a denlike room with what seemed like hundreds of her magazine covers for either intimidation or good PR. Joan was astute enough to know that she (after having graced what seemed like every magazine cover known to man) wasn't about to sign off on a fragrance unless it lived up to her image of herself. And good for her! She was a movie/TV queen of the first order who understood her queendom public and brand.

After the name *Joan Collins' Hollywood* was shelved, I had tried to register the name *Legend*, but it seemed like Ralph or someone already owned it. As discussed, naming a product can be one of the most difficult tasks as many names are already taken and registered. To make a long story short, I then came up with the idea of calling the fragrance *Immortal* and showed her the famous Steichen photo of Gloria Swanson (under a black lace veil) as scrap art. I must say that, at the time, I really did believe in the concept and was disheartened by the reaction that followed. A phone call and typed letter on personalized stationery appeared the very next day at the BHH (didn't she understand it was only scrap art?), saying that the look and name, *Immortal*, was too self-aggrandizing while her agent phoned me and told me he thought the word was a name for the ancients. Couldn't we find a youthful name that wasn't as pompous? Perhaps they had a point!

I flew back to New York a bit disheartened and then back to LA, had another Cobb salad with blue cheese on the side, and prepared myself for what would hopefully be the final (and successful) meeting with La Collins. That, or fireworks. The day arrived, and I sat next to her and her manager and said, "Joan, if I could have named this *Legend*, I would have, because you are indeed a legend, but someone else owns it. That said, I've looked at every word in the English language dictionary (which I did), and since you are truly, *truly* spectacular, that's what I propose to name it." She immediately agreed with my hypothesis, and more important, since it was available, that is what we named it. Now in the end (it was the eighties after all), I really can't remember how spectacular the results were or how long it lingered (was it as big as Alexis's shoulder pads?), but I still have her missive written on her personal stationery that reminds me that enduring movie stars endure because they understand their brand. I recently went online to see if *Spectacular* was still around and there are a number of Web sites featuring "vintage" *Spectacular* and selling it, claiming it as *the* "floral scent recommended for romantic wear," whatever *that* means. In the end, I'll never forget her pyramid bed and the image of Joan and The Donald descending the escalator at the Trump Tower launch party, followed by two violinists as she and her Nolan Miller wig made their way through the crowds and paparazzi.

Say what you want about the launch of *Spectacular* or Joan Collins, she is a star. And nobody does it like a classic movie queen. They're not going around with police ankle bracelets, greasy hair, and no underwear. Joan really deserves the fragrance and the name because she really is spectacular. If they ever give me my own fragrance, I'll take *Ridiculous*. It's not too far from the truth.

*   *   *   *

One of my other all-time favorite celeb stories was when I was handling a superlarge cosmetics account. (Yes, more cosmetics. I've handled quite a few.) The mercurial yet brilliant brand owner hired his celebrity wife's best friend (an Oscar-nominated actress) to hawk a line of antiaging products for the brand. I, of course, had proposed someone else for the product. Someone I thought was known for looking great for her age, such as Kim Cattrall, which I thought was more on strategy. This idea was shot down by Mrs. Mogul in favor of her Oscar-nominated best friend. Now that might sound wonderful on paper, but just because you're an Oscar-nominated actress doesn't mean America *really* knows who you are. Regardless, I was told that the deal was done. And quite frankly, I was surprised that Miss *Uncommercial* would do a commercial. Once I heard that the deal was a multimillion-dollar contract, I quickly understood her "motivation," but given the task of creating a commercial for a woman who a) wouldn't say the product's name in a script, b) would not talk about antiaging in the commercial, and c) wouldn't use or apply the product in any way, wasn't exactly easy.

I, of course, called the mogul and said, "How can I do a commercial for a product when the said actress won't use or say the name of the product and won't talk about antiaging?"

"You'll have to figure it out," he barked. "That's why I hired you. You'll love actress X. She's a good girl. Oscar-nominated." *Click!*

Not to mention the shoot was in less than three weeks.

The first thing I did was to hire a well-known celebrity photographer, who I knew could help make any celebrity comfortable and look good, because at the end of the day, in my opinion, that's *all* they care about—how they *look*. And he was one of the best at it. Needless to say, script after script after script was turned down by the actress's agents, saying we should delete every mention about age. Finally, I confronted her management about why they would never have her say a word about age for an *antiaging* product. "Why would we want to have people think she is older than she is?" they replied. "Then why is she doing an antiaging spot?" I asked in a less than calm tone, only to be told, "I'm sure you'll figure it out." *Click.* Soon afterward, I got the call from the star's agent saying they had wanted her husband, an up-and-coming director (read: not exactly a copywriter), to write the script. When his script arrived, which read like *War and Peace* for a thirty-second spot, it was discreetly canned.

Finally, after weeks of sweating it out, we came up with the idea about inner beauty (hers) and outer beauty (what we do). All very New Age! The mogul's actress wife (now the voice-over, of course!) would read the product portion that talked about antiaging and the product name. Hence, solving the problem that the actress in question would not talk about antiaging product benefits. To my delight, the script was finally approved, and I thought our problems were finally over. After all the drama, I breathed a sigh of relief!

The day before the shoot, her agent called to tell me the great news!!! She was *pregnant* and showing! *Pregnant* for an antiaging product!? I felt like I was living in an alternate universe for the advertising insane. Images of beach balls and adult acne for a skin product danced through my head, proving one can never *chillax* in the ad biz.

The day of the shoot arrived with the star (who, honestly, was perfectly lovely) looking like she was on her way to a mommy-and-me class. Hair, makeup, and a locked-off close-up shot took care of the pregnancy issue (we shot her from the shoulders up). Additionally, we shot the actual product in the next room, as if it didn't exist, and she delivered her lines without ever saying the name of the product or what it did. In retrospect, her agents and managers had been forward thinking, for after she gave birth and was off losing the baby weight, a gorgeous TV commercial was running, keeping her in the public eye. Although sales were strong for the client, we lost the account a few weeks later. Most likely for my being too opinionated and not agreeing with everything the mogul and/or his wife said. Ironically, Mrs. Mogul later got the boot as well, which only proves ad agencies are disposable, but third and fourth wives are, too! Natch!

＊　　＊　　＊　　＊

And sometimes in the ad biz—like any other—roles get reversed. The stars need to look to you for inspiration—or perhaps just derivation. A number of years ago, I was approached by a former client of Dana's, Elaine Goldsmith-Thomas, who was making a movie with Bruce Willis and Halle Berry about the ad industry. The movie, *Perfect Stranger,* was a psychological thriller that had Bruce starring as a suave ad executive and Halle Berry as a reporter-turned-corporate spy. Elaine asked me if Bruce could shadow Jon and me for a day to "get into character." Bruce, to his credit, showed up at kbp and was engaging, asking some insightful questions about account switches, reviews, and the competitive nature of the business since that was relevant to the story line. In one of my favorite scenes, Bruce discovers an employee's disloyalty and throws him across the room and shouts, "I hope they have a job for you over at Kirshenbaum!" as he sneers at the disloyal turncoat. Another scene has him confronting Halle in his car, in a menacing tone asking her if she is a spy for Kirshenbaum. I'm not sure if the ad business is ever as *dramatic,* throwing a disloyal employee across the room and through a desk, but I have known some marketing executives who, when facing a major issue, explode or engage in ridiculous behavior. Whenever faced with a crisis or dilemma, being cool, calm, collected, gracious, and transparent rule the day. Otherwise, it's just another Hollywood movie with an unhappy ending.

＊　　＊　　＊　　＊

While celebrities, in my experience, really only care about what they look like, successful businesspeople (in my humble opinion) care about what people think. Having had the privilege of working with some of America's biggest stars and for some of America's most famous business people has only reinforced my theory. The truly successful business people understand not only their own brand but their corporate culture. They have an intellectual take on how they or their brands should be perceived rather than on an actress's base level of "how do I look?" Having done a branding project for Martha Stewart, I can tell you she really does serve a cake in meetings (and slices it beautifully as well). She is also dedicated to the highest quality products and searching for that essential information, whether it's a new recipe or a new design for her furniture line. Barry Diller, who I worked with when we rebranded the Home Shopping Network to HSN, is as intense and inquisitive as you'd expect him to be (and surprisingly, walked me to and from the elevator). He also has one of the most forward and visionary platforms, having recognized early on the magnitude of home and digital shopping.

Having worked with a number of people who have more zeroes than the rest of us, I have often been asked if the rich and famous really are different. In my experience, they are like the rest of us, just more amplified. The celebrities are more insecure about their looks than we are, and the millionaires and billionaires are more inquisitive, have better manners, and are just plain smarter. Which would you rather be? I'll take the extra zeroes any day!

CHAPTER TEN
IF YOU CAN MAKE IT HERE, BUY PROZAC!

IN A CITY OF RICH people, the old adage is true: Money does not buy you happiness. Some of the richest people I know are downright miserable, on meds, and don't have a nice word to say about anything or anyone. If they go to a swanky charity event, the husband might say offhandedly, "I hate these events. My wife drags me here after a hard day's work. Who wants to be here?" Hello, it's the Plaza Hotel, and you're eating truffles while listening to one of the world's most famous singers belt it out for you and this worthy charity! And you're so blasé and on your BlackBerry. In fact, in the mid '90's I remember one particular charity event where I was seated at a table with a world-famous photographer, a publisher, and the drug-addicted son of a famous actor who was engaged to a fairly well-known sitcom star. There we were, all seated at the table and literally everyone was either too cool or too rude to talk to each other. Not that that was unusual behavior at that time. That is until Liza Minnelli walked over and sat down, and not one person said hello or even nodded. Since Dana was powdering her nose in the loo, after a few awkward moments I walked over and said "I cannot sit at the same table for dinner with Liza Minnelli and not tell 'Liza with a Z' that you are great and I am a fan."

"Dear boy, you're the only one with manners," she replied, motioning me over. "Not to mention you have the best hair!" I did have to explain to Dana, when she returned from the loo, why I was virtually sitting on Liza's lap, having my hair caressed. No one at the table spoke one word to each other during the entire dinner. When Liza got up to sing "New

York, New York" or something from *Cabaret* the actor's son did a face-plant into the mashed potatoes.

Now, not every charity or social event can be as deadly as that but you might hear a socialite say, "Can you believe this party?" (Meaning: The hostess didn't hire her party planner.) And then, about the people, "She looks pretty calm." (Meaning: I wonder if she *knows* her husband's girlfriend just arrived.) Or about her friend, "She's still pretty, I guess." (Meaning: After two eye-lifts, a mini face-lift, and boob implants, she went to the wrong doctor.) Or, "We've been best friends for so long. You should have seen her back in the day." (Meaning: Many meanings. She is either prettier or uglier—depending on the inflections in her voice—or she was a party girl, slut, waitress, or all of the above.) My favorite back-handed New York "best friend" compliment of all time is: "I'm the only one who knows what she *really* looks like." (Meaning: Both a complete overhaul and implies that absolutely *nothing* about her best friend is real.)

As I look back, the city was at its most vulgar and decadent in this environment, right before the financial collapse. Bad behavior was rampant, and Wall Street ruled the roost. In addition to the catty women, there was the constant refrain of the men who felt they were seated at inferior tables at an event or restaurant: "You don't *know who* I am!" (Yes, I do. You're an ass!) And the indulged children, some of whom it was whispered to have flown commercial, were the worst spawn of this set, particularly when the economy set all-time highs. (But they're still all pretty spoiled in New York, in any event.) I am now confronted with children who come for a simple sleepover bringing their portable Wii or have dinner preferences—not just to eat what's being served. My favorite story about this little issue was when I took out my son and his friend (age nine) for dinner, and the kid ordered oysters Rockefeller and a filet mignon! And he actually sent back the filet (he asked the chef to butterfly it!). It is not untrue that my own son asked for a Caesar salad, hold the anchovies, but I *draw* the line at oysters Rockefeller! We soon changed schools.

In this environment, creative people are often looked down upon or ignored by most financial men (obviously, with exceptions, as I've noted earlier). They don't understand creativity or advertising unless it involves a film premiere and a hottie. They think the profession is a hobby. They might say: "Oh, I wish I was in a fun *little* business like you." I stress the word *little* or *fun*. "You ad guys have all the *fun* while *we're working*." Meaning: "I make money with real work, *but* I am so friggin' jealous and want to come on a shoot with all the models." A couple of years ago, I went to a fiftieth birthday costume party where two guys (one dressed as a pimp and the other as the Tin Man) slapped each other on the back and said right in front of me, "So, Phil, you want to buy an ad agency—NOT!" and laughed hysterically. They were shocked when I told them our agency had already been sold (which it was, a forthcoming story).

I think the main message is, for the most part, that financial guys don't get creative guys. Their decorators are tolerated so their wives can have dinner companions and/or walkers. But a seemingly successful creative hetero male upsets the apple cart. In addition, the reverse is true when it comes to the wives. I always get the prime seat at a dinner party, because the wives want to sit next to an ad guy (read: straight, sensitive male with funky hair), while Dana routinely gets shunted off to a lesser seat or table. This summer, we attended a lovely dinner in Southampton. I was seated next to a well-known princess and a socialite while Dana was actually seated in the next room at the *children's* table (with the decorator). I did feel a little pang of guilt when I saw her taking her napkin and making a hand puppet for the five-year-old dressed in Chanel! Meaning: No one wants "women younger and prettier at the main table, but *ad guys are fun!*" If you think this is wacky or insane, this truly is the world where I ply my trade. New York agencies also have something of a mixed reputation. Out-of-town clients know they often have to have a New York agency but are somewhat afraid that the agencies are *too* "New York" and won't understand them and their market, i.e., the rest of America (meaning: New Yorkers are not *real* Americans). However, there can be a bit of reverse snobbery. My mentor, Jerry Della Femina, once told me that he often referred to the people living between New York and LA as the "flyovers," i.e., people you fly over to get to LA or New York. We were once pitching the fashion business from Walmart, and the agency team all flew out to Bentonville, Arkansas. Once I passed the sign outside the prison that listed the number of people incarcerated and a McDonald's (Over a Billion Served), I knew I was in the heartland. Since we were all wearing trademark New York black (as if there's anything else to wear!), the receptionist called the client and without looking up or blinking a fake eyelash under her blue eye shadow said, "The New York agency is in reception." (Meaning: We didn't look like *anyone* in Bentonville, or we had left our short-sleeved poly shirts and slide rules home.)

Out-of-town clients sometimes bring in cost consultants "for the New York agency," and I can't tell you how many times I've heard after a presentation that "the creative work is too *New York*" (meaning: expensive, elitist, overtly sexy, liberal, intellectual and/or non-mainstream enough). New York, though, has become more like Europe than the rest of the United States with its international flavor and level of sophistication. Most of our staff, interestingly enough, is a great international mix of non–New Yorkers. New York is the center of the ad world because it attracts the best talent. I once heard a great explanation that small towns never change because all the really smart and interesting people get up and leave and move to places like New York. Whenever I interview young creative talent, I always give them *more* credit for finding a way to get here because New York is not only tough but expensive.

I recently started a small creative venture called Nuestudio Group. Its focus will be proprietary innovation; new-product development, design, and entrepreneurial marketing solutions at the outset. I decided I wanted to hire a young star as a creative director. I interviewed quite a few people until I met a young guy in his twenties, Miles Skinner, who like everyone his age was covered in tattoos. He hailed from Kentucky and had a fabulous portfolio designing and creating everything from street art to Nike sneakers. I asked him how he came to New York and he told me he wanted to come to New York so badly, he ran away from home when he was quite young. When I asked him how he survived, he revealed he'd sold pot and had been arrested, but not before having quite an operation employing many people in the process. Given New York's tough exterior and the fact that he'd reformed himself, I said, "You're hired! I'm glad you told me and as long as you're not doing that anymore I have no problem with it. After all, part of me is impressed you're an entrepreneur. You're just selling the *wrong* commodity. I'll help you sell the right one." Because I was impressed with him *and* his creative work, he got the job and is now creative director of Nuestudio. After all if you can make it here you can make it anywhere . . . and that's New York for you!

✽ ✽ ✽ ✽

Given New York attracts the best talent but has the most European flavor of any American city, it's not surprising that over the years we have attracted many, many European clients. And believe me, working in Andalusia is far more fun than working in Arkansas.

Ivana Trump once said, "I make my money in the United States and spend it in Europe." Now this is a philosophy that entirely resonates with yours truly. Additionally, having shot an ad with Ivana for Judith Leiber, the luxury brand that makes five thousand dollar minaudières (that's *evening bag* in English, people!), I can say that I also adore those who speak of themselves in the third person. When Ivana arrived on the shoot trailing couture, I steered her to the trailer where the hair and makeup was. She looked at me and said, "Ivana does her own hair." Something tells me her hands alone don't touch the updo, but I took it at face value and handed her a Goody comb.

Me, Ivana, and Nelly on the Judith Leiber shoot

Hopefully, one day, I'll be able to get away with saying, "Richard does this or that." But, in the meantime, I'm totally with the bouncy Czech who *J'adore* vacationing in Europe. Hey, I'll even do Ivana one better: *Not only do I like* making money in the United States and spending it in Europe, I like making money *in Europe* and spending it *in Europe*. Perhaps it feels like that eight-week, five-star hotel teen tour my parents sent me on. There's a certain art to it that doesn't exist as much in the United States, but nobody does it better than the Euros. A little-known secret is that advertising is the *teen tour* of professions. As one of my best friends, Patty, always says (she says she is a *travel whore*), what other job sends you to explore exotic locales and someone else pays the travel expenses?

My first international extravaganza was an incredible trip to Ireland. In the spring of '89, we'd landed the Guinness account, which is an Anglo/Irish brand (or an Irish/Anglo brand, depending on which country you happen to be in at the moment). Most clients want to inculcate and indoctrinate the creative director into their brand, which often translates to *"Hello, field trip!"* As I was the creative director, they arranged for a two-week, all-inclusive pub crawl to Ireland and England for me, and off I went on Aer Lingus (which proved to be a winner. I loved the emerald green brand color and shaving kit giveaway). Once in Ireland, they assigned me a wonderful tour guide whose name was Declan. Declan had the Irish twinkle in his eye, and Ireland proved to be a revelation. My mother was a scholar of Joyce, and there seemed to be a pub and a bookstore on every corner reminding me of her reading *Ulysses*. The Irish were friendly, and like the Hewlett fish store, they loved a great smoked salmon, so I felt right at home off the bat.

The purpose of the trip was to understand the DNA of the business, and although I thought Brandpa loved his brands above all others, in Ireland, Guinness was the equivalent of the Statue of Liberty. Who knew a beer would be a tourist attraction? I asked myself. From the moment I got in any taxi, hearing the driver probe, "Have you had a Guinness?" to the sensuality of the way the people described it, "The thick, rich creamy head will *melt in your mouth*," etc., I could not get over the *cult* of Guinness.

I have never seen a country or a culture so incredibly involved with one brand. It was as if the entire country was transfixed or in a coital trance over stout. Not to mention that, according to my memory, no one seemed to eat *anything*. People seemed to exist only on *Guinness*. The thick, dark liquid was damn good, but no one in the Five Towns ever *ate* a beer for lunch or dinner! Where was the buffet or the carving station? Where was the corned beef or sliced turkey with mustard and cranberry relish? Where was the pig in ze blanket? Finally, in a remote pub on the northwest coast, I begged Declan to get me something to eat. We walked into a musty, old pub that felt more like a gothic church, where the bartender was in the usual rapture about the Guinness on tap. Again, I heard the usual litany about the thick, creamy head; I felt like I was in a beer porno. Finally, I looked at the blackboard and asked what was for lunch.

The bartender looked at me seriously because I had hinted at food. "We got a cheese sandwich."

"Anything else?" I asked, not thrilled at the prospect of a wilted cheese sandwich.

"I got a ham sandwich."

"Anything else back there?"

"I got a cheese and ham sandwich," he deadpanned, which only added to the ambience and my hunger.

Still, Ireland with its lush green-carpeted lawns, quaint cobblestone streets, and bittersweet, misty landscapes moved me. We even wrote a poster, which is somewhere in the Guinness museum, with the headline, "The beer you've been practicing for." Dublin, before the boom, was a quaint, gorgeous town with weather I would describe as the "four seasons in one day." One minute, it would be Hamptons weather, the next minute, freezing, raining, or broiling. On a pub-crawl of the countryside, I visited a three-block radius, which I was told constituted the "Jewish community of Ireland," I walked into the lone Irish kosher bakery and asked where all the tribe was. "They've all moved to the suburbs," I was told in a lilting Irish accent by a man named Murray. (Not surprising, knowing my peeps.) Additionally, the beer experience paved the way to subsequent trips to France for Moët & Chandon and Hennessy and to Italy for the Tuscan wines of Ruffino. It was all wonderful and marvelous but like my teen tour, totally spoiling me for la dolce vita.

*   *   *   *

The boardrooms of America are stocked with (if you're lucky), soggy tuna sandwiches, a bag of chips, and a can of soda for lunch. Europe, on the other hand (not withstanding my culinary experience in Ireland and Eastern Europe) was a culinary orgasm. Let me describe to you a business meeting in France or Italy for, let's say, a first-rate wine client.

On arrival, you're welcomed to the château or villa by an elderly English expatriate couple who live there just for the sole purpose of greeting guests and being utterly charming with their kindly eyes and bad sturdy shoes. A brief tour of the vineyards and facilities and the aged presses "gets everyone in the mood" for a good meal. Lunch is served either in a hall of mirrors à la Versailles or served al fresco under an ancient ilex. Business is initially *not* discussed, as you munch on small dishes of quail-egg-size olives and fresh potato chips (in France) or olives and broken pieces of Parmigiano cheese (in Italy). The host or hostess then welcomes one into lunch or dinner but not before offering a glass of red or white, or a flute of champagne, for good measure. Although one might expect Russian service in such surroundings, it's more likely to be a bit more low-key, such as antique silver serving platters circulated by the well-trained, silent staff to place the everyday Limoges on. The main course is often followed by a soufflé or freshly baked torte, and espresso with *vin santo*. It's disgusting as everyone in Europe is stick thin to boot!

After retiring to one's room at the Relais & Châteaux or villa for a nap, one then returns for a two-hour (at the most) strategy meeting before dinner and/or a club. Life is grand as one samples veal *aux champignons* with a first course of champagne risotto. Polite conversation is made with the charming aristocratic owner of the *maison*, who is one of the few people who can get away with wearing his watch on top of his shirt cuff à la Gianni Agnelli.

Apart from ordinary meetings, when one is on photo and/or TV shoots, agency personnel stay at five-star hotels and enjoy the local gastronomies with the clients. Ah! *Les pauvres.* One has to bite the bullet and invite the clients for a drink, dinner, and then the eventual five-star wrap party where we all toast to the commercial's success and all the *hard* work and how difficult the director or hairstylist was. This usually takes place the last week of July before the European clients take the *entire* month of August off, and I mean *off,* not to be seen or heard from till September, regardless of any crisis at hand. I am referencing the halcyon days of client spending, before the great recession and those pesky cost consultants. Although everyone is more economical these days, the Euros still understand you have to pay for the "art of it," and I admire that. And they still value good ole American and New York gumption. American ingenuity and innovation are what Europeans and other cultures prize, so why not live it up in Europe as we give it up! No matter what the travails or the day's business, there isn't much to complain about after a shoot when they show you to the Marlene Dietrich suite at the George V. Somehow it just feels more fun than eating at Chili's in the airport in Columbus, Ohio (although I do love Chili's chips and salsa).

CZECH, PLEASE!

Eastern Europe has consistently proved to be a culinary disappointment, sadly. But first, I must explain that there are a few places to get a great deal on a commercial shoot. Spain, Prague, and Brazil figure into the ad agency production circuit where you can get the best deal on production and/or buy out the talent (for the layman that means not having to pay out residuals), and there are professional, local crews set up to service American and European clients who want a great deal.

It was in the 1990s, and we were shooting a commercial for our champagne clients, Moët & Chandon. There was a hot director who I recommended, and we all agreed that Prague offered the client the most bang for the buck. We came in on budget, and like my teen tour, I was once again packing for an eight-day tour-of-duty, this time in the somewhat newly opened Czech Republic. Sadly, there wasn't a George V or Beverly Hills Hotel of Prague, and I was going to have to rough it at a small deco-style pension operation that was more hostel than hotel. And I'm certainly *hostile* to *hostels*! For my taste, I knew I was in for major trouble when the heat didn't work and all I could get to eat was strudel. (That said, everything else was shit but the strudel—a wonderful apple tart with a delicate crust and powdered sugar—was *beyond*.)

At first, Prague proved to be a virtual feast for the eyes. We would shoot in the mornings, and in the afternoons and weekend, I would tour the historic spots. Now, I've always been a bit of an antique hound. Anyway, to make a short story out of a long one, it dawned on me that Prague proved to have more antiques per square foot then I'd ever seen in one location. If a store was selling watches, it didn't have five or so watches; it had five hundred. I went on a shopping binge until I came to the realization after visiting the Jewish ghetto that the watches I was buying (which were all circa 1942) seemed to me like Holocaust loot. I became nauseous and immediately gave them all away. After this epiphany, we left Prague. And for the second half of the shoot, a broken-down bus took us to some broken-down castle and film studio in the middle of Bohemia.

Besides being freezing—and I mean gusts of icy wind whistling through broken walls and infiltrating my camel hair coat (which, by the way, was very Rick in *Casablanca*)—the entire film studio was filled with anti-Semitic graffiti, i.e., lovely sentiments like *Jude* and *Kill all the Jews,* etc. (The film company didn't even have the good sense to whitewash or take it down.) It had obviously been a hotbed of Nazi propaganda during the war, which, of course, made me extremely comfortable!!! Lunchtime proved to be a feast of *treif* (long gray sausages that resembled *you know what*) and sliced ham in a chafing dish. You bet I was chafing! With nothing to eat, I subsisted on bread and water. Needless to say, I couldn't wait to get my ass out of there.

The biggest joke of all (and quite fitting) was the models we hired for the TV commercial *didn't know how to smile*. I kid you not. When the director asked them to smile, they sat frozen as if being interrogated. Perhaps the genetic imprint of the war and Communism had whittled down their humanity, and every direction was met with "How much?" The one time someone did smile, her teeth were so in need of an ortho-dontist, we had to hire and bring in models from the UK (as *if Britain* is the center of good teeth?). Prague was so depressing, I made a hasty exit to the airport only to find out that we had a flight delay. It was the one time in my life I was looking forward to *airplane food.* (Actually, that's not true. The egg omelet on Delta still makes me salivate). Once at the airport, I begged the woman behind the counter for the next flight out so I could get something to eat. The horrified woman looked like she was disappointing me by letting me know that there were no flights to the United States. Only to Russia, Poland, and Germany. Only to the Eastern Bloc? I wasn't about to go to a place half my relatives tried to get out of a hundred years ago! Crestfallen, I told her I hadn't eaten anything but apple strudel for ten days, and she took pity. After much checking, she found me a flight with a stopover for the night in Copenhagen, and then to New York.

I happily boarded the flight, and the moment I stepped off the plane, I was in a land of happy, smiling, good-looking people. It was if I awoke in a wet dream. I checked into a small suite in the D'Angleterre, which was dedicated to King Christian X (who wore a Jewish star during the war to save his Jewish citizens). It was like coming home to a bowl of steaming matzoh ball soup! The wonderful concierge encouraged me to try a new restaurant that was known for innovative Danish cuisine, which proved to be a winner (as opposed to phallic-looking gray sausages). I sat next to a table of young Danes who not only looked like they were out of central casting for an Abercrombie ad but invited me to dinner as well. Besides the company, the presentation was Danish modern cuisine: all perfectly symmetrical in its freshness and brilliance. Small toasts with cylindrical vegetables and chicken proved to be a party in my mouth as I marveled at Danish civilization.

When I finally got back to the States and into the editing suite, the actual commercial suffered a bit due to the cast of the *unsmilers,* but who could blame them. After all, if you had bad teeth, lived under Communism, and wore cast-off Members Only jackets from the eighties, you wouldn't be smiling, either.

CHAPTER ELEVEN
THE BEST STUFF DOESN'T GET ANY BETTER!

IN EVERY CAREER, THERE ARE defining moments or greatly missed opportunities. We knew from the beginning that Snapple would be one of those. Sometimes you are presented with an opportunity and you give it your all. Clearly, we knew something was in the air with this new, innovative product, and we would do anything and everything to get it.

Hymie, Lennie, and Arnie: the founders of Snapple. How can I describe them? How can you not give credit—enormous credit—to three guys who created one of America's greatest brands? Talk about street smart. Look up the definition, and you'll see Hymie Golden, Lennie Marsh, and Arnie Greenberg, followed by their wives.

It didn't hurt that the Goldens, the Marshes, and the Greenbergs lived in the Five Towns. All I had to mention was the corned beef from Woodro's deli in Hewlett or some Hawaiian chicken and a potato latke (fried to a golden brown with kasha knish), and I was "in"! Before I even tell you about Snapple, every party, office function, or Snapple gathering was like an over-the-top bar mitzvah. The three friends had struck liquid gold, and they wanted to party hearty *Five Towns–style*! (And no one does it better than a posse with some new money to burn from Hewlett Bay Park.) Besides being blinded by Mrs. Marsh's diamond, which could power Manhattan with solar energy, people were really happy for these honest, smart, lovely, charitable guys who hit the big time. They were mensches of the first order, and they would give us our biggest platform to date.

*　　*　　*　　*

So there I was, judging the Wendy-the-Snapple-Lady look-alike contest at the first annual Snapple Convention. I peered into the audience at the more than 3,800 people who'd packed Hofstra University in Long Island. People were strolling through the Snapple Art Gallery and snapping photos of the art consumers had sent in that they'd made from Snapple bottles. There were games made from Snapple tops, among other things.

I'd seen some pretty wild stuff since starting the agency with Jon, but this ranked as one of the all-time kookiest of days. Say what you want though, it proved the point that Snapple meant more to its consumers than just being an iced tea or lemonade. It was a community, a brand they held close to their hearts and minds. People stopped to hug and kiss Wendy and ask for her autograph. The founders, their wives, and kids all had photo-ops and we all congratulated one another on such a successful, innovative event that got press from *Newsday* to the *Evening News* and attracted consumers from as far away as Puerto Rico and Canada, who'd flown in for it.

I always say that when a great campaign meets a great product, great things can happen. The Snapple convention was indeed a "happening." When people ask me why Snapple was such a great success, it's because the founders did everything "their way." And since they had an innovative groundbreaking product, they knew intuitively they needed innovative and groundbreaking advertising and marketing. They also knew enough to get the right people to do it for them and not get in the way. Very often, people stop me and say how much they still love the original Snapple ads and Wendy, or are surprised when I let them know I discovered her in the mailroom. How did we do it? How did we get there? I've also been around plenty of agency people who point fingers at the creative work when we didn't win a pitch and I always smile at their naïveté. That's because you can't look at creative work or the creative people doing it in isolation. Before you can get to great creative, you need great direction, or what we call in the ad biz—a great *strategy*.

Sometimes it's intuitive; sometimes it's not. But unless you have a killer strategy, you might go down the wrong path creatively. In the ad biz, you very often have to "pitch" your ideas and "pitch" your reasoning for strategies to get potential clients, and you are most often competing against other agencies doing the same thing. A pitch consists of putting together a pitch team of people who have a passion for the category and brand. Before you get to the creative work, you need to formulate a pitch strategy for the brand and business. Then the fun stuff—the creative stuff—falls out of a pitch strategy.

Pitches are very labor intensive and can be extraordinarily expensive these days, costing upward of a hundred thousand dollars for a large piece of business, including travel. I have always bristled a bit at pitching, because unlike other service industries, like architecture or interior design, in which the companies don't really design and build the house first (unless they choose to, stupidly these days, on spec) and give it away before they get hired, in the ad biz, that's how it's done. You have to bite the bullet and do it, because everyone else is! One of the great struggles in being in a creative business is convincing people or clients that ideas are as meaningful and legitimate as a factory or commodity. Most people have a hard time comprehending that the *intangible*, i.e., brand vision, helps create the world of the brand. And very few people succeed at capturing and creating a world consumers can aspire to and actually enter. Ralph Lauren is the apex of this philosophy. When you see Ralph and or step into one of his stores, you are entering Ralph's world, a place most people aspire to.

The pitch strategy for Snapple was incredibly smart and thoughtful. Rosemarie Ryan, our head strategist, who would later become our president, worked with Jon and our planning team to create the strategy "100 percent natural" marketing. Snapple was a new category of product. Since Coke and Pepsi couldn't claim a natural strategy, we could and did. The creation of this strategy had meant "brand sleuthing"; interviewing the staff, spending time at their office in Valley Stream, and trying to figure out what made the Snapple culture so unique. I know in the advertising business laymen get confused between a strategy for the brand and a tagline. A tagline like "Coke Is It" or "Made from the Best Stuff on Earth" is a line consumers identify with—it makes them relate to the brand. A strategy is a road map to get there. So, again, "100 percent natural" was a guide, *not* a tagline, and we applied this natural "filter" to everything the brand would care about or do. And what it wouldn't do. That is what made the process unique and led us to great work. As an example, if other companies paid a celebrity to endorse the brand, which essentially is artificial, Snapple would use one of its *real* employees in its campaign. It had to be real and natural, and it was this filter that would help keep Snapple, Snapple.

One of the great things about the ad biz, in my opinion, is getting to know not only the categories you're working in, but also the brands, their histories, and the founders, CEOs, or current management. I remember visiting the fabulous Château de Saran, the home to Moët & Chandon and Dom Perignon. When we first were awarded the business, I asked my client if I could see some of their historical labels. Since the brand dates back to 1743, they led me up a back set of staircases to an original attic to look at eighteenth-century labels, typography, and the like. We actually ended up using this as an inspirational guide for our work. Going up in the attic in the château was a profound moment for me. It really was a branding education. Now, not every brand has a château, lineage, or brand elements that date back to the 1700s, but if it's a successful brand, they each have an individual culture worth understanding and discovering. I coined the term *brand attic* and instituted a search for brand identity and culture for each client, whether they had the lineage or an original attic, or not.

From the moment we were awarded the Snapple business, we knew we were witnessing the birth of a great American brand. Not only did consumers love the product, but they were protective over it and felt like "Snapple was theirs." They didn't want anyone messing with it. When it came to the packaging, consumers tested in focus groups would say things like "Oh, poor little Snapple, they don't really know to do sophisticated labels." They'd shake their heads, going on, "But don't change a thing." They loved the naïveté of the design. From the beginning, the founders of Snapple seemed to trust their intuition and do everything right. The original inspiration for the bottles came from their grandmothers mixing lemonade and ice tea in old-fashioned jelly jars, they said. The founders would say "no bubbles up the nose with a regular-shaped bottle for our consumers." They brilliantly hired Howard Stern to help sell and seed the product with his stalwart consumers. He romanced his love for Snapple with a dedicated and powerful audience.

One day, Rosemarie Ryan and my executive CD, Bill Oberlander, came to me and said they'd found a box of these letters from consumers. They were unlike any letters they'd ever read before. We read some of the letters, and they said things like "I love Snapple so much I'm getting a Snapple tattoo" or " I'm going to name my baby's middle name Snapple." Brandpa would have been proud. I went out to Valley Stream to see if they had a customer service group who were handling and answering all these amazing letters, and that's when I met Wendy.

*   *   *   *

Wendy Kaufman, a.k.a. the Snapple Lady, is truly one of the funniest people I have ever met, and I should know since I've been around a lot of funny people. I've written comedy for Joan Rivers, worked with funny people like Anne Meara (she did a reading of my play), Kristen Johnston from *Third Rock from the Sun* (she did too), Henny Youngman, Tony Roberts, and Woody Allen himself. Not to mention Lois Korey, who wrote for Ernie Kovacs in the 1950s. Just like Ed McMahon was blessed with a radio voice, Wendy is blessed with the funny gene. The moment I met her sitting in Snapple's office answering every letter with warmth and a sense of humor, I knew something special was there. The fact that she, too, was a Five Towns girl did nothing to diminish my love for her and we consistently meet at delis where Wendy (and I) sample the wares and compare them to Woodro Kosher Deli in Hewlett.

Since the strategy team came up with "100 percent natural" advertising, Bill Oberlander and I and a wonderful young team, Risa Mickenberg and Amy Nicholson, concocted a campaign where the letters were read and actually answered on air *live*! Hymie, Lennie, and Arnie loved the soon-to-be-famous letters campaign the minute they saw it but had no idea we were going to recommend Wendy as the person reading and answering the letters on air. Since the commercials had to be real (hence, 100 percent natural, and *hello,* this was before there were reality TV shows), Wendy needed to be *the one.* If the truth be known, Wendy was the obvious choice, but there were obstacles to selling her (and in anything that's successful and different, there always are). The idea of a heavyset woman being the spokesperson for a natural beverage company concerned everyone and had never been done before. The fact that Wendy had the crazed Long Island accent, was a real Jewish broad, and had been in drug rehab didn't help matters, either. The founders had thought someone more mainstream and attractive—like Pam Anderson or Loni Anderson—was more like it.

We gave it a long hard think on how to sell Wendy. Finally we came up with a plan. The idea was to compare Wendy to the two most popular women in America at the time. So we brought in big blow-up photos to the marketing meeting and said, "Oprah and Roseanne are the most popular women in America, and both are full figured. And the average woman in America is a size sixteen. Everyone will relate to her and, most important, it has to be real. And Wendy is *real.*"

Arnie Greenberg, who is an incredibly astute and shrewd business-man, said, "Well, if you guys want to, fine. That's why we hired you." He then added, "But if it doesn't work, we'll fire you." With those words, we set the new Snapple campaign in motion and, as we said, *everything* had to be real. We even chose a young documentary-style director, Steve Kessler, so the commercials would have a documentary-style feel. One of my favorite spots was of a woman who wrote in that her dog, Shane, would come running every time she opened a bottle of pink lemonade. The day of the shoot, she kept opening bottle after bottle with that famous clicking sound, and Shane just lay there like a log. It was our deci-sion to run the spot the way it was, and we ended up showing a close-up of Shane's cute face as he just lay there. It was really funny. Another spot was of a young boy who wrote in to see if all his favorite Snapple people who wrote letters were real, and we shot a commercial having them all show up at his house proving they were. The look of surprise on his face was priceless. Again—reality TV? You betcha!

As for Wendy, she became a phenomenon and went on every talk show known to man. She is still ranked as the number-sixteen most famous spokesperson of all time. (Even though she has been off the air for ten years.)

Thomas H. Lee, who hails from Boston and is one of the great businessmen, gentlemen, and venture capitalists, bought Snapple, took it public, and sold it to Quaker Oats. Having seen and been through companies in transition, I can honestly say there is an entire book in how Quaker managed to buy and lose something like $1.4 billion on Snapple. I was there and witnessed the destruction firsthand (including the snide remarks questioning Wendy's relevance despite her popularity—I promptly put the gossipers on notice). All in all, it shows what happens when a large corporation buys and dismantles a brand culture. I'm not sure how many millions they lost when they decided to pull the plug on Howard Stern, who helped put the brand on the map in the first place, but they didn't think he was appropriate!

Honey, I'm going to make you a star!

Appropriate! He only helped build the brand they bought. But it doesn't take a rocket scientist to know it can't be good to piss off a public advocate, and it was wild when he started calling the brand *Crapple* on the air. My prediction is someone will "get smart," rehire Wendy, and get a Harvard case study on the re-rebranding of one of America's most recent success stories.

All in all, Snapple was one of our great moments. All the stars aligned, from the incredible founders to the innovative product, to Wendy, to a campaign that took risks and started reality trends. Snapple also taught me the value of not just consumers but *cultists*: consumers who adopt brands, care and nurture them, and hold them close to their hearts. It's one thing that corporate America still doesn't fully understand. It is getting a good beating as brands competing not just on price or benefit but for the hearts and minds of consumers are winning the day, especially as the rise of social media (Facebook, Twitter, and YouTube) influence them. Consumers are controlling, commenting on, spoofing, and creating dialogue about their favorite brands in ways previous advertisers could never have dreamed of or controlled. Social media is and will continue to redefine the advertising world.

Brands now have a life of their own, and company culture is becoming ever more transparent and important. It's one of the reasons why this outsider, renegade brand shook up the cola wars, by creating an insurgent war—one they fought on their own.

There is something truly wonderful about the "being there" for the rise of a meteoric brand. You feel like you're on a roller coaster going all the way to the top. It's just not as much fun to be there on the way down! Lennie and Hymie and Arnie may have started out as window washing and health food store company owners but no one can say that this wasn't one of America's sweetest success stories. And I'm proud to have had a part in it and taken a gulp!

SHOPPING IN THE AD JUNKYARD

We were always very amused when we would come up with truly a great idea and a client *wouldn't* buy it. At first, when I was quite young, it was baffling. How could they *not* buy it? Then I understood, the world is really broken into two client groups: "those that play to win and those that are playing *not* to lose." The not-to-lose crew always wanted safe "benefit"-oriented work, and certainly, there's nothing wrong with that. But, at most, it will get you a double or a triple but not a home run (to use overused sports analogies). And not everybody wanted what we were selling!

Jon and I always said we should recycle the campaign ideas and sell them. Since we were so busy, we just put them aside into a place in file cabinets (and the file cabinets in our minds) and called this space the ad junkyard. Every so often, we would troll the junkyard for a pitch or a client, and a few of the agency's most famous campaigns were often stashed there first and recycled. One of the first was a campaign we created for the designer Albert Nipon and his diminutive but fiery wife, Pearl, who I quite liked. They wanted to see new work. But, in the end, what they really wanted was a refreshing of their well-known campaign with the tagline "The Nipons were there." I have to hand it to Pearl; she at four feet eleven inches had no problem appearing in a hunting scene next to five-foot-eleven-inch models. The Nipons were there all right—in the ads. Pearl and Albert turned down a wonderful idea, which promptly went into the ad junkyard. I actually did go to see Pearl before we recrafted the idea to ask her if she would mind us using it for another client. To her credit, she said no. The recrafted campaign actually worked better for Coach, and we soon launched "The American Legacy" campaign featuring descendants of great Americans and their Coach bags.

Before the innovative design talents of Reed Krakoff, we were charged with contemporizing their iconic handbag, which consumers often termed (at the time) their *mother's handbag.* The campaign, featuring the descendants of famous Americans including George Washington, Daniel Boone, and Paul Revere, really broke through the clutter and helped cement Coach as a classic American brand while connecting it to the future. I now call it the perfect bridge campaign, between what was and what would be.

One of our all-time favorite stories was how we recycled a campaign and actually won a big piece of business because of it. The amazing and beautiful Valerie Salembier (who is now publisher of *Town and Country*) was at the time president of the New York Post Company, owned by Peter Kalikow. We met Valerie through the late, great Jerry Nachman, who was the archetypical newspaper guy. We had this great idea, which was on top of our ad heap called the Three Biggest Lies in New York. Since, as you know, I'm from Long Island, and I always took the Long Island

Railroad to and from the city, I noticed that (in those days before it was chic to read the *Post*) people were embarrassed to read it on the train and would actually slip it under a *New York Times*. Hence the idea "I never read the *Post*" was featured in the ad as the third lie. The three biggest lies were: "My commute is only twenty minutes," the *Post* line, and my all-time favorite, "It's only a cold sore." We believed the ad would create unbelievable attention for the *Post* and the agency (which it did). But first, we had to sell it.

Walking into Valerie's office was almost out of a movie. Tall, statuesque, and blonde, she was a woman running a newspaper company, which, at the time, was really a good ole boy's club. Before she saw the ads, she said, "Now, Jerry wanted me to see you, but I've already awarded my account to another agency." When we laid the campaign on her desk, it literally took her breath away. And to her great credit, she immediately called Peter Kalikow and said, "Peter, I have something here I really think you need to see." Valerie, you see, was a forward-thinking, innovative chief who was playing to win!

When we went to see Peter Kalikow to show him the campaign, I made the mistake of laying the portfolio case on his conference room table, which was the largest table I'd ever seen. "Please remove that" he said in a way that made me think he was going to push an ejector button and propel me out the building. Kalikow looked at the ad and said (just as Arnie Greenberg had said regarding the Snapple campaign), "Fine, but if it doesn't work I can fire you with a clean conscience." Is that a favorite client quote or what?

To Valerie, Jerry, and Peter's credit, they hired the agency and ran the campaign, and it was a huge success. The self-effacing humor and wit of the lies helped to take the sting off the *Post* and create a high/ low approach with its customer base. We learned to use this treatment with many mass-branding accounts, to great effect. We also learned and understood one of the most important business lessons: No one, let me repeat, no one, but no one was handing out new accounts to us. In fact, it was the reverse. We were actually (at that time) the harder choice to hire. Did we cry? No. Did we fold? Absolutely not. We decided to make it difficult *not* to hire us by actually offering up ready-made creative ideas that were too good to pass up. If a client didn't want it, we'd change the garnish and serve the tasty dish to someone hungrier. Now, people often say we've been lucky—and we have been (thank G-d). But sometimes you need to make your own luck, too! And we never lost our own hunger, this scrappiness, no matter how big we'd become.

We also seemed to visit both the ad junkyard and brand attic for hotels, among other things. I named Kalikow's newest real estate hotel tower, calling it the Millennium Hotel chain. Strangely, I never asked or got paid for it! A few years back, the agency pitched the Wyndham Hotel chain, which is a moderately priced hotel chain with some very nice properties. Wyndham was in search of a new agency and new positioning. Our team once again looked in the brand attic and our planners found an interesting, yet small-scale program called the "ByRequest" program. Wyndham had its own program differentiating itself by offering a few custom options, such as one could order a foam or a feather pillow, request a certain soft drink, etc. We thought using "ByRequest" was such a unique strategy that we decided to center the entire pitch around it, blowing out the "ByRequest" program as its core offering.

We knew "ByRequest" was a fairly risky pitch strategy as in order to really execute well, Wyndham would have to hire "ByRequest" managers for each location and step up and further invest in the service. We also felt we would need to help them set up the program and train their employees. In the end, we were awarded the business and created the marketing program. We even ran the "ByRequest" form as the newspaper ad. Our TV commercials were also breakthrough with attendants setting up special rooms with themes like blackout shades for Dracula. Within a few years, Wyndham had millions of "ByRequest" members, and my friend Steve Rudnitsky, who was CEO at the time, credits it for helping build their business. Truthfully, all we did was take a fresh look at some of their preexisting assets and remarketed them.

It might look easy in retrospect, but getting a client to buy and sell a really big idea into their organization takes a brave client who knows they will reap the rewards if it's a home run but will also have to take the hit if it strikes out. (For a non-athlete, how am I doing with the sports analogies?) Not every client is equipped or has the stomach for the game. But when you get a client who sees value in a big, hairy, audacious idea, you really need to appreciate them—even more so because it's so much safer to take the easy, boring route. Adding a difficult economy to the mix (and the thought that if the idea *doesn't* work, they will perhaps even be out of a job) makes it even more crucial, when selling an out-of-the-box idea, that it is a great one. It also goes to prove that a great idea has a life of its own. Someone may decide they don't want it or aren't brave enough for it but just like Grandma Elsie always said, "There's a cover for every pot." And there's an idea for every client. It's just finding the right match. Whether it's hot off the presses or lurking in the ad junkyard, when a great idea hits, you can sit back and enjoy the fireworks. And that's one of the best fringe benefits of the ad biz. A great idea needn't go off into the ad sunset, but may live to see another day. And *that's* not a lie!

CHAPTER TWELVE
THE MOST FUN YOU CAN HAVE WITH YOUR CLOTHES ON. OR OFF!

ONE OF THE GREAT ATTRIBUTES you need to be a successful ad guy or gal is to be quick on your feet and always offer up service with a smile. It's part and parcel of the advertising toolkit to acquire and retain clients. I've also been told I'm a creative director who is also about account service. After all, let's not forget the client is paying your bills, so I have always believed our clients do deserve respect. And to be truthful, I've always been lucky in that I've enjoyed my clients. And there are a great many lengths the successful agency guy or gal will go to service the client. I actually think the advertising business is a fabulous, underrated business. To quote my dear friend and mentor Jerry Della Femina, "It's the most fun you can have with your clothes on."

That said, I have taken my clothes off for a client. Here, let me explain.

It was our first big print shoot for our first really big account, Hennessy Cognac. It was 1991 or '92. (The eighties had just ended, so who can remember?) We'd been hired by the venerable importer Schieffelin & Somerset to handle the Hennessy account. And since it was our first breakthrough account, we wanted to do everything we could to succeed for them. Which we did, apparently, given the account stayed with us for sixteen years, as I mentioned. A long-term, loving romance.

I'd found this breakout young photographer, David LaChappelle, who I touted to the president/CEO of Hennessy, Penn Kavanagh, as being the next Avedon. Jon and I called Penn our "Medici client," since he nurtured, supported, and sponsored young agencies and creative people. He had a keen eye for the emerging young talent and was a formidable,

151

elegant, and distinguished patrician gentleman. The type of man who looked like he could run for president and you'd vote for him.

I invited Penn downtown to Area (or some such club of the era) to see David's latest installation, since Penn wanted to see more of his work before using him. As it turned out, David's show, as I foggily recall, consisted of a singular photograph. It was of a large erection that wrapped around the ceiling of the club, in black and white. "Interesting choice of material," Penn remarked dryly. However, David's regular photo book was lush and elegant, and Penn signed off on him to shoot what we would later term *the feelings of* campaign.

Our research had told us that the cognac consumer, at that time, had been aging and it was important to invite and encourage a new generation of cognac drinkers. Since cognac is an acquired taste for new drinkers, the campaign we devised was meant to simply make visual analogies to what is a sensual drinking experience. In the first ad, we showed a couple in a sensual kiss, with the copy "the feeling of Hennessy cognac." The second ad showed a woman wrapped in silk with the same copy.

The visual element of the campaign called for sensual black-and-white photographs contrasted by the cognac's glorious amber liquid in two side-by-side snifters. Since the art direction of the ads also needed a European sensibility, we shot the kiss ad first, in New Orleans, in a gorgeous old arcade that looked a bit like the rue de Rivoli in Paris.

We then traveled to Mississippi, where we found a wonderful old plantation to shoot the "wrapped in silk" ad. I cannot underscore the importance of this shoot and getting it just right. The account exec was with us, along with the Hennessy ad director, Ben Stone. We were quite lucky to have him. A social, smart guy with a trademark handlebar mustache, Ben approached everything with incredible professionalism and a sense of humor. Which as it turns out, was needed—and greatly appreciated by us.

So there we were on the day of the shoot, and the weather had turned gray, cloudy, and rainy. There was a lake on the property, and David, the photographer, had suggested we shoot the model, naked and wrapped in a yard of silk fabric, standing on a rock overlooking the water. He thought it would look iconic and sensual. We all agreed. We thought the photo would be gorgeous and that the singularity of the proposed image would work well in the layout.

There was only one problem. The model may have been gorgeous, sultry, and exotic, but she wouldn't come out of the trailer. As I've said, sometimes in order to get a client to buy into a concept, you need to persuade them, but not fight with them. In this case, we had to work hard to persuade the talent, not the client. And by the end of the day, most of us would have been happy to have picked a real fight with her. Usually, hair and makeup can take two to three hours, so at first no one thought anything was amiss. But after three hours, it became apparent that either the model had passed out, or she wasn't coming out for some unknown reason. I went up and knocked on the trailer door. The conversation went something like this:

"Um, excuse me, but you've had the entire crew waiting for over three hours, the weather is getting worse and we're losing light. Can you come out of the trailer?"

"I'm not coming out."

"You're not coming out? Why not?"

"I'm naked!"

"Didn't your agent tell you that you'd only be covered in silk?"

"Not on a cold, rainy day. I'll freeze."

"Listen, what can I do to make you feel comfortable?"

"Nothing. I'm not coming out."

The word spread. "She's not coming out," everyone was whispering and hissing.

The photographer talked to her through the door. Jon talked to her. Ben talked to her. The account guy talked to her. She just wouldn't come out. Finally, I knocked on the door of the trailer once more.

"Is this because you're naked, or cold?"

"Both."

"Do you want me to clear the set?" Meaning: Shoo everyone away except for David.

"No, that won't do it."

"What will?"

"The only way I'm coming out is if everyone gets naked, too."

Naked in this weather! No way, I thought. Not in front of *my* client. Not happening. However I was open to a bit of negotiation. "That's not fair. You have some fabric around you. How about if we strip down to our underwear?"

"That's fine."

"Fine." I couldn't believe what I had just agreed to.

I talked it over with everyone and said if we wanted to get the shot, we all had to comply. Off came my coat, my sweater, my shirt, and my trousers. She even wanted socks off. I must have looked like quite a sight with my long hair, shivering in my Calvins and my red high-tops, which I wore sans socks. (Well actually, I did think the red high-tops were a good look.) To Ben's credit, he stripped down, too. We all did to save the shoot. Finally, the model crept out of her trailer and made her way onto the rock, in all her glory, with the wind whipping the gray silk around her.

I knew we'd have a nipple problem, but retouching could fix that. What couldn't be fixed was the arrival of the Mississippi police. They

She finally came out of the trailer before the cops arrived

saw an exotic naked model on a rock, being photographed by ten white guys in their underwear. They blasted their sirens.

I looked at Jon. "You go talk to them. They're not going to get my hair."

Jon, of course, went over and, in a good-natured way, managed to explain the situation, helping us all avoid arrest and being thrown into a Southern prison. He was always quick on his feet in situations like this.

Needless to say, I learned my lesson. If you're in a client service business, you have to want to

154

serve. And if it means dropping trou to get the model out of the trailer, well, so be it.

Over the years, I've gotten so good at what I call account service—and service with a smile—that I've actually applied it to my personal life. It's a relative's birthday? I send flowers. I do it for my clients, so why not a close relative? I actually recently gave a friend of mine advice when he was having issues with his parents. I said, "Instead of getting angry and into a fight, why not just give your parents some *account service*. You don't get angry and in a fight with your clients, so why not apply the rule to family. If it's a birthday, send flowers. Talk to them in a respectful tone. Get back to them if they call you. If you can do it with a client, I am sure you can do it with your mother." You don't have to be best friends, just honor them by giving them client service!

A few months later, I ran into him and complimented him on a new solid gold Rolex.

"I have you to thank," he said. "All these months, I've just been following your advice and doing what you said and giving my parents client service and look what they bought me for my birthday."

"What do I get," I joked.

"Your advice is solid gold, so I'll pay for drinks," he said. "However, I keep the watch."

You need to remember first and foremost that the ad biz is an account service business. You aim to please. You need to really care about your clients, believe in their products, have integrity, and use your creativity not only to make spectacular brands and create breakthrough marketing, but sometimes to salvage or resurrect those same brands. And you need to feel comfortable doing all of this. Sometimes, just sometimes, with a smile on you face and your pants around your ankles.

THE LANGUAGE OF CLIENTS

In order to be good at the ad business and serve your clients well, you need to speak a foreign language. I often refer to this skill as "client translation." Most agency people live to hear themselves talk, but I know that one of the most valuable tools in our biz is being able to *listen* and translate what the clients are actually saying. Or not saying. Clients come in all shapes and sizes. Some are direct, and some are more shy by nature. Some are expressive, and some you have to pull direction from. Since the advertising business is a subjective business (especially when it comes to creative work), not everyone agrees or has the same taste. Not everyone has the ability to listen and to translate what the client is saying into actionable direction. And not everyone can get and keep accounts.

One of my favorite anecdotes had to do with the way people on one team can see what the client is saying—or what they mean—very differently. Many years ago, the agency had a small furniture retailer in New Jersey called Huffman Koos. Our creative director at the time, Andy Spade, wrote one of the most memorable creative lines for this retailer which I still love all these years later. The line was "Huffman Koos. Where you'll never think, what was I thinking?" It basically sums up most retail purchases. A few months later, I drove out to see the client and present some work with the account executive and junior account executive. When the meeting concluded and we were walking to the car, the junior account person said, "That was a great meeting. They seemed to love everything." The senior account person said, "I'm not sure. I got the feeling they weren't exactly thrilled, but it was an OK meeting." I looked at both of them and said, "Unless we get back to them with their changes tomorrow, I think we will lose the account." Which we eventually did. Everyone *hears* things differently or *wants* to! Or cannot listen and process due to the level of their experience alone.

I have also found that most people have to be told to manage problems up. For the most part, it is human nature to keep problems to themselves. People only want to tell their superiors positive news. It's the rare bird who raises a hand and says, "Hey, I think we have a problem on our hands." I've heard this expressed two ways. My father tells a great story about the son of a very well-known businessman with whom he worked who went to the best Ivy League schools and was very social. Every day and every night was a party, a cocktail, an event. Until one day, the company started to go into a downward spiral. My father said the heir apparent apparently put all the issues, problems, and mistakes into his desk drawer and went off to another party, until a few years later the company finally went out of business. Alterna-Dad always sums this up by saying, "You never know what somebody's keeping in their drawer." I have always wanted to know what the problems were so we could solve them in advance. Jon invented a great term for this: *spotting an iceberg.* We've always asked our people to give us an iceberg alert because like an iceberg, you can see it in the distance, but you only see the top of the problem. And if you can't see the deeper problem, SOS!

I've also felt that spotting an iceberg and alerting the client means you're not an alarmist but that you care. I can't tell you how many times I've uttered the words *excuse me for caring too much*! In the end, clients know and love that you listen and care. In fact, one tip in a service business is that I almost always call an important client from vacation. As in, "Hi, Client X, I'm here in Capri and had a thought for your business." You can't imagine how much of a deposit goes into the relationship bank when you call a client from vacation. It takes very little to do, and it's much more thoughtful and meaningful than a snow globe!

THE LAND OF MAKE-BELIEVE

A few years back, a friend invited me to Sotheby's when Princess Di was in town auctioning off her dresses. For some reason, I went, most likely, like everyone else who did, to catch a glimpse of the most famous woman in the world. Sometimes celebrities appear smaller in real life than they do in print, but Di was outsize and in Technicolor. She radiated health, happiness, and star quality. I could not get over how tall and good-looking she was. Her smile also seemed to light up the room. On my way back from making a phone call, I happened into a side room that immediately became filled with Secret Service–type guys. All of a sudden, Princess Di appeared and all the doors shut, like out of a scene from *Mission Impossible.* Nobody said a word. I looked at the secret service dudes; they looked at me. I looked at Di. She smiled. I smiled. After a few awkward moments, I turned to a man with an earpiece.

"Excuse me," I whispered, "is there a reason why we are all locked in a room with Princess Di?"

"Security reasons."

"I realize that, but what is everyone doing here?"

"What are you doing here?"

"I don't know."

Now, being stuck in a room with Princess Di, when nobody said a word, felt more like being in a room at Madame Tussaud's. That said, for one of the few times in my life, I was at a loss for words. Perhaps it had something to do with the fact that besides looking *unbelievable* in a baby blue glittering somewhat mini dress, her legs came up to my head.

"How much longer do we have to stay locked in here?" I whispered.

"Who knows."

"Is there an issue? Like someone's trying to steal the dresses?"

He refused to answer. I looked over at Di. Di looked at me. She nodded. I nodded and smiled. Was I supposed to say something? I didn't feel it was appropriate to make a joke like when I was introduced to her former sister-in-law, Fergie, by Phyllis George.

"It's a pleasure to meet you, Duchess." I said. "And you are?" she asked. "Richard Kirshenbaum. A Jewish American prince." She laughed, and it made the gossip column in the *New York Daily News*.

Phyllis George, Fergie, and the prince, Richard

All I thought to myself (at the time) was, why bother saying hello? She's Princess Di and she's on top of the world. And I'm just an ad guy who comes up to her bikini wax.

After what seemed like an eternity then, the doors opened and the surreal moment ended, but what I didn't realize at the time was that—at the time—I had no idea Princess Di's life wasn't as perfect as it looked. In fact, she was what I have always referred to as the down escalator. Let me explain. I have this philosophy that in life you're either on the *up* escalator or going *down*. You're never standing still. Now every once in a while, you can get off in the lobby, mezzanine, or go from the top floor to the basement, and/or vice versa. But the lesson is essentially: It isn't what it always appears to be, especially in New York.

Not too long ago, Dana and I were invited to a society gala for the ASPCA at the Plaza. Dana was seated next to the famous movie producer Marty Bregman, and many people stopped by the table to kiss the ring of the man who brought the public movies such as *Scarface* and *Sea of Love*. Suddenly, I saw my old ad accountant (Ken Starr, the one who's in jail for a Ponzi scheme, can you believe it?) walk over to the table. Ken walked over to Marty and gave his respects. It really was a *Godfather* moment as Ken (who I always thought had a bad vibe and a bad overbite) was dressed in a trademark black suit, black shirt, and black tie like a Mafia don. Not to mention that his third wife had been a stripper and her headlights were beaming. Now I haven't worked with Ken or Starr & Co. in more than a decade (thankfully), but I turned away. I just didn't want to engage him. And besides the all-black getup, I sensed he had a black cloud around him. A number of days later, he was arrested for pulling a mini-Madoff Ponzi scheme. His wife directed the police to the closet where he was hiding.

Like people, brands also go up and down on the brand escalator. No two clients or issues are alike, nor how you navigate their issues. One favorite story happened during one week when we saw and presented work to two clients. One client said, "I hate surprises. I want to know what you are presenting before you present it to me." A few days later, the other client said, "I always want to see surprises. Like in a Cracker Jack box." All within the same week. The worst thing is when the company has their own surprise for the agency—when corporate leadership tries to create a smokescreen and pretend everything is wonderful. They put ad agencies in an impossible position if we can't spot the iceberg. If the company purposefully doesn't want us to—or if they are being hoodwinked themselves—what can be salvaged about a brand in such circumstances? It's always the biggest shock when the cover up and the smokescreen are the actual choices made to cover up crises—whether by a couple or a company. If they try to create an image of perfection when there are serious issues at hand, it's akin to shoving the public down the escalator head first when the real truth is revealed. Our agency shot Tiger Woods in an ad for NetJets, and even the styling and the clothes he wore were as asexual as one can get, hence setting up the public for an even bigger tumble. The public doesn't like to be Tiger Woods-ed!

Like real, vulnerable people, the best brands get out there and let the world know there are product issues, the way a couple might let their friends world know they're having marital problems. Or that there has been some financial mismanagement or that a brand is on the road to recovery through image resuscitation. Like just the way it's been public that Goldman Sachs is creating a public campaign to help restore the corporate luster. People like an honest dialogue, they like up-to-the-minute information. Whether you're on your way up or down, honesty is the best policy when the @#*% hits the fan. Crisis management and how you handle the bad news is just as important as all the good things a brand wants to say or stand for. Just because you're wearing an Izod shirt and a pair of khakis doesn't make you squeaky clean. In the end, if you don't manage things, you might get bitten in the derriere by the very alligator you're wearing.

HAVE YOU EVER SEEN AN AD FOR AN AD AGENCY?

Service with a smile includes making your client feel that they have hired the best possible agency, of course. And that means some ruthless self-promotion on the part of the agency if the agency knows what they're doing. Well, maybe just a bit of self-promotion at any rate. I would venture to say that most people have seen lots and lots of advertising, but most likely they've never seen an ad or a promotion for an actual ad agency. Even when I was in my twenties, I always thought that was the ultimate irony. Now, most ad agencies will tell their clients they're experts on building someone else's brand, but they don't know how to brand themselves. We've been called many things by our detractors: publicity hounds, PR whores, ad brats, and the like, because we believe in what we do. In 1987, we created the agency's first ad. It was a black-and-white photo of two brass balls, and all it said was, "It takes three things to do breakthrough advertising. Great ideas are one of them." The ad sparked a great deal of industry conversation and was part of building our brand and image.

**It takes three things to do breakthrough advertising.
A great idea is one of them.**

kirshenbaum bond + partners **160 varick street | new york, ny 10013 | 212 633 0080 | www.kb.com**

The first ad we ran about ourselves

We once even took out a billboard near our office that said "Welcome to Soho! Home of inspiring galleries, charming bistros and shamelessly self-promoting ad agencies, like Kirshenbaum Bond + Partners." Last summer, I was in Paris and stopped in to say hello to Maurice Lévy, who is by far one of the most powerful admen in Europe. Levy led the Publicis Groupe for more than forty years. As we chatted, he remarked that out of the thousands of agencies (and there are exactly 8,250), we were one of the few in the United States that actually built a brand. My scrapbook is full of articles and covers (*Wired,* the *New York Times* Sunday Styles section, *Crain's* Forty under 40). Just giving you the proper propaganda.

While it is crucial for an agency to make a mark and get press, an agency has to also know how to balance getting no press and getting too much press (as clients can also become upset if the focus is on the agency and not them). Every client wants to feel like they're number one and that you're also working for them, not just for yourself, *bad ass*! In fact, in 2000, I was proud to be inducted into the American Advertising Federation Hall of Achievement, along with other recipients like August Busch IV (a long way from Long G'Island beeatch!).

A long way from Long G'Island

I received the Jack Avrett Volunteer Spirit Award for public service. Many of my friends and clients took out ads in the journal, and our Citibank American Advantage client took out an ad that read "This maybe the only time a client is thrilled to know you don't just work on their account, Citi AA."

My wife, Dana, has two great stories: one that illustrates this point, and the other that was critical to her success as a businesswoman and also to kbp.

After six months of dating Dana (this was in 1991), I had to admit I was pretty smitten. She danced on tables, did shots with me at a black tie party at the UN, played footsies with me under the table at Shun Lee, and looked smokin' in black velvet and pearls at a family wedding. I didn't quite understand Dana's strategy because, at times, she could be aloof. But within a matter of months, I had broken it off with the two girls I was dating (Dana says now she maneuvered them out of the way). I also let her redecorate my apartment, by virtue of the fact that one day I came home to her moving out *every* piece of vintage art deco furniture because she didn't like it. I was going to get mad at her for not asking, but there she was confidently directing the coffee table and French leather chairs out the door with the furniture mover and a clipboard. When I asked her what she was doing, she just said she'd gotten me a great price for it all. (Actually, the antiques dealer who took everything just happened to go belly-up, and I never got a nickel.) Still, I found her incredibly madcap and rewarded her with a gold emerald-ruby-and-sapphire bracelet for all her efforts, which could be the ugliest thing I ever bought her, in retrospect. Dana would agree. She hates jewelry.

I think what attracted me most to Dana was her self-confidence and ability to think big. I knew I didn't want Dana to get away, but I also wanted to see if she was more than girlfriend material, and nothing is better than traveling together to figure that one out. Since she was only twenty-four at the time, I did have to convince her mother to let me take her to Europe, but it wasn't too shabby of a trip: the Villa d'Este on Lake Como, the Hassler in Rome, Le Sirenuse in Positano, the Quisisana in Capri. If we weren't meant for each other there, then it wasn't meant to be. Dana was and is the most gorgeous girl (now woman). More beautiful than any model I ever worked with, and smart to boot! I always describe Dana as Angelina Jolie in *Mr. and Mrs. Smith*. She's a knockout who will take you out with an AK-47. Just to give you a sense of how gorgeous she is, during our vacation, when she tried on a bikini in Positano, thirteen young boys clamored by the store window for a peek in a virtual near riot. And in Capri, a gentlemen of about fifty actually fell to his knees in front of his wife and kissed Dana's feet! I kid you not.

I remember one particular afternoon vividly. We walked hand in hand up the Thousand Steps from the beach to our suite in Le Sirenuse in

Positano, which is a glorious villa perched over the Mediterranean with the Li Galli islands floating in the distance below our window. Dana and I were relaxing in the late-afternoon sun on the terrace, having a glass of *prosecco* when the phone rang. Dana had been expecting a call from the Film Society of Lincoln Center. Before we left, she had interviewed to get the job: the head of public relations. I heard snippets of the conversation and thought it sounded promising with questions like "How much?" and "When would the start date be?" After finishing the conversation, Dana strode out to the terrace. She looked like a Bond girl with her flowing waist-length dark tresses and bikini and high heels. "Well, I got the job," she smiled.

"Mazel tov!" I jumped to kiss her.

"Not so fast. I turned it down."

"What?" I almost yelled. "You turned down the head of publicity for the Film Society of Lincoln Center? Why?"

"Because I'm not interested in independent or art films," she said nonchalantly. "I want *blockbusters*."

"What? But you're only twenty-four."

"And you were only twenty-six when you started your own business."

Dana has a frustrating way of always being maddeningly right. However, I still thought a twenty-four-year-old junior account executive *pisher* shouldn't turn down such a prestigious position, especially as a jumping-off point. Either Dana was the next Sherry Lansing or she was loony. I couldn't decide. Regardless, her decision had me questioning her judgment. The trip was divine and quite a whirlwind. But in the back of my mind, the jury was still out on whether she knew what she was doing.

Two months later, Dana and I were having salmon teriyaki and plum wine at Japonica (one of our favorite watering holes on University Place) when she told me she had gotten and accepted a job to work for a well-known Hollywood publicist, Nancy Seltzer, who while having quite a tough-as-nails reputation handled some of Hollywood's biggest stars. Dana would go on to work with everyone from Sean Connery and Harrison Ford to Susan Sarandon, Nicole Kidman, and Julia Roberts before eventually starting her own company. She had gotten her block-busters, and I knocked myself for doubting her. I proposed shortly after.

The lesson I learned from my twenty-four-year-old fiancée was to set audacious goals and always follow your dreams. Don't take no for an answer and don't always say yes to the first offer.

*　　*　　*　　*

I learned even more from Dana once she was running the New York office of the PR firm. She was handling the publicity and had organized a press tour for one of the world's biggest movie stars. On the way to an appearance on Letterman, a paparazzo snapped a shot of the two of them (from behind), which appeared the next day in the *New York Post.* The very *next day,* Dana left the house early in sweatpants, her hair in a pony, her glasses on with no makeup. She still looked gorgeous but clearly dressed down. I asked her why she was dressed that way and she responded, *"The greatest movie star* saw the photo in the *Post* and isn't talking to me." In the photo (and real life), Dana is much slimmer and looked prettier (in my opinion) than her client. Hence, the silent treatment. Dana was smart enough and shrewd enough to understand that she wasn't going to be successful if she overshadowed her client (despite the fact that the movie star is a great and unusual beauty) or if she even gave her a run for her money.

So Dana went out looking like a sweat hog to keep Miss Movie Star happy. And do you know what? After that, the greatest movie star only wanted to work with Dana until Dana retired when we had kids. It taught me an important lesson. Get press, get PR, but don't overshadow your client or have them think their ass is twice the size of yours!

AND NOW: A WORD TO AD WIVES ABOUT AD LIVES

While Dana has retired, she can't (or at least hasn't chosen to!) retire from being an adman's wife. And she is the best at it. Most people don't really understand or know that a successful adman/woman needs a serious ad spouse (nowadays, ad partner). I've often thought being an ad wife/

spouse/partner can be trying. Vacations are interrupted at every turn, family events are blown off, cell phones go off at the most inopportune times, and you're constantly on call (like a doctor) to take a visiting client and their wife out to dinner or to the theater. You have to be dressed to the nines (but not overdressed), coiffed, (but not intimidating), and interesting (yet not overstimulating), especially to client wives or client spouses/partners. Briefings often take place in the corporate car on the way to the event (the client's wife's name is, the kids' names are . . .).

Now, no one is throwing a charity dinner for my wife based on the job specs. But when you're in a client service business, there are times when your life is not your own, and you have to rationalize bad behavior and client intrusions. When we first married (after I dragged Dana to the first ten client dinners and deadly industry events), she actually turned to me and said, "I don't know if I signed up for this." Somehow I got her over the hump. After all, her work as a publicist meant we were and are very well matched. That said, she has been incredibly supportive and confident through all the model and celebrity shoots. Every once in a while, though, she'll pull a "Dana"—like the time she showed up (in a trench coat and sunglasses) to the bra-and-panty fashion show in Florida when we were handling the Maidenform account. I had told her not to come, that it was just another "boring work-related trip." Yeah, right! All of a sudden, I look up and Dana is sitting in the same row as I am, taking "notes" on the models walking the runway in bra, panties, and high heels. Like a scene out of *I Love Lucy*, Dana sat down and turned to me, lifting her sunglasses.

"Oh, just another boring work-related trip!" she smirked.

"Well they *are* wearing panty hose for modesty," I meekly countered.

If you're married in the ad business and your spouse is not supportive, it can also prove to be difficult. It is not untrue that I, myself, have moved twenty-two vacations in twenty-three years and have actually left the family at resorts during pitches, which can be trying for all involved. Even if you are the one who gets to be away, the thought of exotic locales and all those restaurants in LA you "have to go to" (while your spouse is home changing diapers) can also be trying if you're not in sync. I have seen smart, seemingly well-adjusted ad spouses go bonkers after their significant other is ensconced in a four- or five-star hotel for ten days on a celebrity TV shoot while they are home doing homework with the kids. While I consider myself to be a considerate husband (I buy flowers, gifts, and remember anniversaries and birthdays), there have indeed been a few things I have *majorly* slipped up. After all I am still an adman.

The story I am *least* proud of and now embarrassed about was *so* bad I honestly don't know how I turned from my usual considerate self into a complete unthinking boob. That said I am still a *man* and capable of such things. I am almost too embarrassed to put this on paper, but I'm telling you everything else so why not this? Anyway, there we were in the hospital room after Dana delivered our youngest daughter, Georgia Rose, and she is in her hospital gown hooked up to an IV and trailing the IV on a walker. All of a sudden, I get a client call related to one of our largest pieces of business. The president of the company was on the phone. I do not, to this day, know what came over me (we had visitors), but because of the noise, I shooed everyone out of the room. The last thing I saw was Dana pushing her IV down the hall as I went into client mode. Needless to say, WWIII did occur. Hopefully I have made it up to her, but I will never live it down! And I still feel badly to boot.

All in all, you do have to be confident to be an ad wife or partner. I've seen all types of ad wives and different ad lives often result by their behavior. If you're considering marrying an adman and/or an adwoman, please consider the following archetypes and implications before you agree on a trip down the altar.

AD WIFE/SPOUSE/PARTNER TYPES:

1. The Perfect Ad Wife or Spouse: You are supportive. You hardly ever come to the office. You *never* scold your spouse based on his/her schedule or changeable schedule. You are always perfectly coiffed like Mrs. Draper and know how to mix the perfect martini, while swaddling a baby and saying "Of course, that's fine" while he/she misses your anniversary due to his/her business trip.

2. The Nag Ad Wife: If you are resentful that your ad spouse is forced to eat at Nobu and stay with clients at Shutters on the Beach in LA, perhaps the ad business might drive you and your spouse both insane.

3. The Intefera-Yenta: If your wife is strolling the baby into the office *while* you're in a client meeting and doesn't get that the meeting needs to continue after a quick "Oh, isn't it *so* cute," you've already stayed way too long.

4. I'm Riding (So Low) on Your Coattails: How many times must an agency indulge your wife's or hubby's work-related passions (and fantasies)? I've seen it *all* over the years: indulging spouses by using them for catering, invitations, hair and makeup, styling, accounting, PR, photography, helping them become agents, actresses, and even offering up yoga! Eventually, you have to stand on your own Manolos. You've come a long way, baby, not on your husband's (partner's) coattails.

The smartest thing Dana has done is what she *hasn't* done. Which is most of the former. She only comes into the office once a year and hardly anyone knows what she looks like, except my clients. One year, she came to the Christmas party, and everybody thought I was having an affair because Dana doesn't look like anybody's wife or mother. Her lack of need for affirmation among my staff is what has made Dana not just the perfect ad wife, but the perfect wife.

All in all, being an ad wife or an ad hubby can actually help or hurt. I have seen a number of employees' wives/spouses actually hurt their husbands'/wives' careers as they've been too assertive or actually dismissive of their spouses in my presence, joking about their spouse's shortcomings. I've seen househusbands or boyfriends (one I recall could hardly speak English) stroll into the office and try to take control or offer uneducated opinions or negotiate contracts. I have seen families try and take advantage of the most inane things—and *try* to put the weirdest things on expense accounts. No dice! If you or anyone you love is an ad wife or hubby or partner—do yourself a favor if you like the ad business and want "in," get your own job in another agency! And take a cue from my perfect, wonderful ad wife. Everyone *does want to see you*. At the holiday party!

CHAPTER THIRTEEN
ICE, ICE, BABY

I FOUND BEING ENGAGED FUN. I called it "dating with presents." Like most people, we were toasted and feted by our families and friends, but eventually we got down to business, i.e., getting the ring and setting a date. It is quite true that as women age, their jewelry tends to get bigger. Particularly, because they generally can afford more—and then, as my dear friend and jewelry aficionado Muffie Potter Aston always says, "For distraction as one gets older." That said, after making the rounds of a few diamond dealers, we actually settled on a 4.5-carat emerald-cut ring for Dana. While an emerald- or square-cut ring looks smaller than a round, there was a side of me that thought that a 4.5-carat ring was a bit large for a twenty-something. However, New York City is not the land of understatement! Even the high WASPs bust out the occasional golf ball–size diamond. Weirdly, after all these years, the ring looks small to me now, as the jeweler, Jacques, said it would. So either I need a stronger prescription or my ego has gotten bigger. You decide!

New York hotel weddings are still considered the gold standard by everyday standards. While there are those who will rent out Yankee Stadium for a bar mitzvah or the Metropolitan Opera or the Temple of Dendur at the Met for a wedding, there's also been a Marie Antoinette backlash associated with such lavish displays, and the Plaza or the St. Regis are still considered major, yet tasteful, places for a major event. Perhaps it was one too many weddings or "affairs" at Temple Israel in Lawrence (which is actually a quite beautiful 1920s structure) or at one of "the country clubs," but at that point I was clearly in my "I'm over

Long Island" stage and immediately booked the St. Regis rooftop. My only requests to Dana were that we wouldn't have a wedding video or an ice sculpture, the hallmark of a typical Long Island or *Sopranos* situation! Dana convinced me about getting a video, saying it would be great to document the grandparents, but she agreed with me that there would be no ice sculpture. Needless to say, I thought an ice sculpture was very *Goodbye, Columbus,* and I was having none of it, given my new feelings of urban sophistication at the time.

The day of the wedding in July of 1993 arrived, and Mitchell, my best man, made a concerted effort and offer to have me ditch the whole thing and fly off with him to Europe. The moment I saw Dana, any anxiety I had dissipated. She looked like Audrey Hepburn with her upswept hair, long gloves, and empire-style wedding dress. Everything was so incredibly beautiful, from Dana to the thousands of roses (from Stefan's in Cedarhurst), that it was actually quite romantic. I felt glamorous in white tie and tails. As the big moment came, the orchestra started, and I started down the aisle. Only then did I spot it!

My blood ran cold as out of the corner of my eye I spotted the *largest* ice sculpture known to man (of two intertwined swans with our initials D and R, carved out of one formidable piece of ice, holding caviar to boot!). I almost passed out. It went something like this:

"Will you, Richard, take Dana to be your lawfully wedded wife?"

"There's an ice sculpture in the house!" I whispered.

"I know," Dana smiled. "Isn't it great?"

"And do you, Dana, take Richard . . ."

"How could you do this to me?"

"Oh, relax. How could you have a wedding and no ice sculpture?"

"I do."

What I didn't realize at the time was that was exactly why I was marrying Dana. She was gorgeous and madcap and, in the end, she always keeps me real. Now as I look back on the wedding all these years later, I am so deliriously happy I *had* an ice sculpture because truthfully, who am I *not* to have it? It's what the crowd wanted; even the Gentiles thought it was great. I mean, if you really think about it, how could you go to a real

Jewish wedding and have no ice sculpture or PIB (pigs in the blanket)? It would be a travesty since they're such crowd pleasers. It's like those Chinese restaurants that try to be classy and won't serve fortune cookies. It's such a letdown and actually heartbreaking at the end of your meal! And Brandpa loved the wedding. The pigs in the blanket hit the spot! After he died, I found he kept the room service menu he saved from the hotel for breakfast in which he had ticked off Tropicana orange juice, Quaker Oats oatmeal, hash browns, Canadian bacon, and Wonder Bread white toast, butter, and yes, you guessed it, Maxwell House and half and half, living up to his Brandscape.

*   *   *   *

After all these years, I've come to realize that embracing your truth is integrity and if you deviate from who you are, you become disconnected from people and what they want and actually expect. Everyone, every community has its own cultural ice sculpture and if you run too far from it, you realize you're just running away from yourself. As Grandma Elsie always said, "You need to keep the best and leave the rest." I have learned and seen that all of this holds true for companies: If they deviate from their roots, their culture, and what they represent to their community, then they've lost their ability to sell themselves with honesty. Without integrity, they lose traction, and without traction, they lose their power.

Similarly, where creatives are allowed to become subjective about a brand they are working on, they often deviate from the brand's core equities. A few years back, we were awarded the Meow Mix business, by a brilliant and passionate entrepreneur named Richard Thompson. Jon and I knew he was an original when we saw the title on his business card, which read "Top Cat." When we were first awarded the business, I asked to see a historical reel of all the commercials to date, and do you know what? The famous "Meow, Meow, Meow, Meow" jingle (which has 94 percent ad awareness) had not been used in sixteen years. I scratched my head and couldn't believe it. Actually, I could, but was stunned that no one had brought back (or wanted to) one of the core equities of the brand and one of the most famous jingles in all of advertising. The first thing

I did, creatively, was to embrace the obvious. I took the jingle out of the brand attic and modernized the jingle. We did it by doing a VH1 "pop-up video" version of the commercial and then set out to find ways to utilize the jingle in fresh new ways. Richard Thompson's brilliant leadership, product innovation, and our marketing helped reenergize the brand, and it was sold for two and a half times what it was purchased for just fifteen months prior. Thankfully, Jon and I participated in a small but meaningful way, financially. As I look at it, the jingle was Meow Mix's ice sculpture. And once the company went back to its core, it became successful because that's what consumers *expected* and *wanted*.

*   *   *   *

I recently took my kids for brunch at the famed institution on Amsterdam Avenue and Eighty-sixth Street, Barney Greengrass. They sell the best bagels, lox, and sturgeon in New York, which is saying a lot, and eating there is stepping back in time. With all the Italian, Asian, and Mexican food my kids are eating, Dana and I thought that (as Brandpa would say) "a little Jew food would be good for 'em." While we were paying the bill on the way out, Gary Greengrass, who is one heck of a nice guy, was standing behind the counter and said "Happy New Year, Richard, I hope it's a good year for both of us. You're in *advertising* and I'm in *appetizing*!" And, boy, is he in appetizing.

The exchange does bring up a point that the best, the very best businesses I have both encountered and worked with *know* who they are and *know* what business they're in. I realize it sounds pretty easy, but lots of people get sidetracked: some out of making the wrong strategic decisions, bad advice, and a few out of sheer boredom or greed. Part of being in the ad agency business is to help clients both realize and commit to a macro strategy. Strategies can affect every part a business operationally and if the company and brand is clear on what they are, they'll have an easier time having clarity in all areas of decision making. That's not always possible, though. For instance, years ago, we handled the advertising for CNBC under Roger Ailes, which was and is a fabulous business-oriented channel. Only problem was, at the time, one of its biggest shows had nothing to do with business but was called *Real Personal* with the host Bob Berkowitz. We had many, many discussions about taking on an *all-business* positioning (which it eventually would). But at the time, CNBC loved the revenue, and it wasn't about to go cold turkey by canceling the highly rated sex show. The channel couldn't commit to a brand strategy at that time, and we understood.

It's also understandable that in an economic downturn people generally stick to their knitting. It's when the economy is experiencing a boom that you not only see more unfocused behavior but people doing the strangest things generally for ego, fun, or greed, which are never great motives. Alterna-Dad always says, "People generally make bigger mistakes when business is good rather than when business is bad." Over the years, I've gotten to know quite a few well-known families that are in what Alterna-Dad also called dumb businesses (not dumb as in stupid, but non-glamorous, non-exciting businesses that throw off a great deal of cold hard cash). Instead of appreciating the goose laying the golden egg, some family members get bored and sell or even trade their shares for more glamorous climes, like the music, the movie, or the restaurant business, or disastrous all-stock deals. Only in retrospect, do they appreciate the non-glamorous but profitable business they were once in. We once handled one such company that was in an extraordinarily mundane category. The great-grandfather started it, and three generations had lived quite well off of it. We were awarded the business, not once but twice, by the very capable and conservative CEO, who knew as much about the business as the sons and grandsons who owned it. The second time they hired us, we went out and staffed the company to give it the highest level of service. Until, that is, the grandson called me and fired the agency on the spot. It turned out the fabulously wealthy family was looking to sell the business and wanted to cut expenses rather than invest in the company. Now under many circumstances, it's never pleasant to lose a piece of business, but the jerk actually fired us and refused to pay the ninety-day contractual fee, which is fairly standard in our industry. And we had a signed contract to boot. Since I knew the grandson socially, all I said when he refused to live up to the contract was, "I'm not going to take you to court on this, but I lay my head on the pillow at night knowing I did the right thing. I'm not sure how you do it." He told me he slept just fine. He yanked away the account knowing we would have to de-staff and pay severance to the team *his* CEO asked us to hire. They had plenty of cash to have done the right thing.

Now I am sure the family is richer having sold the company, but it didn't surprise me when I picked up the newspaper a while back and saw the grandson probed on illegal trading tactics. What this family didn't understand was that they would have been possibly richer by reputation handing down a third-generation business to their own kids, and by honoring contracts rather than the resulting negative PR.

On the opposite end of the spectrum, our clients Andy and Carrie Kozinn owned their third-generation business, Saint Laurie Merchant Tailors. Was it Prada? No. Was it profitable? Yes. And we did a great job helping them succeed.

As I walked out of Barney Greengrass. I looked up past the stuffed sturgeon hanging on the wall and saw a sign above a family portrait that said 1908–2008. Gary Greengrass was still standing behind the counter, welcoming guests and ringing them up the way his father did and I am sure his grandfather did. Knowing who you are, what you do, sticking to your knitting, delivering on a great product, and treating people with respect is not only the way to success, it's—what's that word again? Appetizing!

＊　　　＊　　　＊　　　＊

The value of integrity, and of self-awareness, has been critical to the success of kbp from an internal perspective, as well. People often ask Jon and me how we've managed to have been such good partners for twenty-three years. This, of course, not only figures in the wins or the losses of accounts, but multiple marriages, family additions and losses, as well. Given all the potential possibilities for disagreement, I would venture to say that, first of all, you have to be lucky if you go into business with someone who is fundamentally honest and if, despite your many differences, you can arrive at a meeting of the minds when both sides express different views and feelings. As Alterna-Dad always said, "It's not the *problems*; it's *how* you handle them." The basic premise is first understanding whether you enjoy each other's company and bring different skill sets to the party. It's amazing to me when I often hear people looking for business partners who are exactly like themselves (as if they honor only their strengths and feel a mirror image is a more flattering scenario). I would vehemently disagree. The *more* different you are, the *more* the different set of skills you and your partner will bring to the party. And the *more* it's going to be a kick-ass party—and a memorable one at that. The thing that matters most is the common thread of integrity, and how you navigate conflict and/or view the world.

A year into our business, Jon and I met a very talented art director whom we were considering for partnership. We worked together well and we needed his skill set at the time. As I've recounted, both Jon and I *love* great food and wine, and the initial business was all about lunch in good restaurants (and how to afford them!). It was also limited to an hour (before we had to get back to our real day jobs). When we brought the intended art director to lunches with us (where Jon and I would order half the menu), he would always order the cheapest thing and a soda or say he'd eaten before, and then want to split the bill down to the penny. After the third lunch, Jon and I looked at each other and said, "No way!" How could we go into business with someone who didn't seem to enjoy food and wine? It was more than lunch but a philosophical issue. More importantly, we felt that if a person was cheap with food, they might be cheap and petty in business. Not interested! So we sent him packing.

That is the philosophical point of going into business with someone you see eye-to-eye or stomach-to-stomach with. As different as Jon and I were and are, we invariably order the same thing off the menu. Now that's a real partner in my book!

As it relates to working out major business issues, Jon and I stumbled on a formula that served us well for more than two decades. In the beginning days of the company, when Jon and I were looking for real estate space for our first real office, I was a bit nervous about 1133 Broadway. Jon said, "This is it! We have to take it." I gave him all the sound reasons for not plunging into a multiyear lease for a brand-new company. Jon countered, "We need the space for new business and growth. I am a hundred percent." Since I was waffling on the issue, I gave it to him. He seemed so confident.

A few months later, Jon wanted to hire a well-regarded (but in my book, *not* entrepreneurial) account guy. After hearing his list of demands, I marched into our shared "non-office" and said, "There's no way we can hire this guy; his list of demands is a mile long for a small company. I don't get it and I'm a hundred percent he's not the one."

Since I was 100 percent and Jon was 75 percent, he gave it up to me, and we agreed not to hire him. Hence we institutionalized what we called "the 100 percent rule." Our feeling was and is, it's unlikely that if a person is *really* honest, he or she cannot feel 100 percent about the same thing (for the most part and excluding Middle East politics and/or other tinderbox issues like abortion). If one person feels 100 percent and you feel 99 percent, you have to give it up to them, and vice versa. I cannot tell you how important the 100 percent rule was in avoiding and resolving conflict. I'm not going to lie to you and say we never got annoyed with each other, but no matter how different we were or are, we always arrived at the right place. And we always prided ourselves on trying our best to do the right thing. Additionally, Jon and I also never made the other person feel badly or small if their gut was wrong.

Jon and I at our El Morocco party... It was great fun. I'm 100 percent!

We just moved on. We rarely used the 100 percent rule, never abused it, and many years later, even let our then-president, Rosemarie Ryan use it, as well. It has *always* worked. Now, sometimes in life or in business, there are things that are out of your control, and for those things, I call it "being in an impossible or difficult situation and trying to do the best you can." But if you truly do your best, then that's good enough in my book. We may not be Internet billionaires, but to quote Alterna-Dad, "At the end of the day, all you have is your name. And whether it's a good one or not is up to you." And on that issue I'm 100 percent!

CHAPTER FOURTEEN
IN THE NAME OF LOVE

THE YOUNGEST PERSON I HAPPEN to know is Alterna-Dad. Last year, in characteristic fashion at his eightieth birthday party we threw for him at Le Cirque, he raised his glass and said, "I love life. Here's to my next chapter." For a man who had lost two wives and has had his share of serious surgeries, I've never once heard him complain. I always say his optimism has been greater than any material gift.

In 1989, a year after my mother, Marilyn (a.k.a. Maude), suddenly passed away, my father met and married a divorced woman from Great Neck, Long Island. Phyllis Trinin was younger and very attractive and in some ways a lot like my mother—opinionated and caring—and this came through in her job as a social worker for underserved teens. Nevertheless, the death of a parent is different than a divorce. And despite my father's happiness, I had mixed emotions at the fairly hasty union, which I guess, in retrospect, was normal. In my father's defense, he became engaged to my mother after dating her for only six weeks in Fire Island, so a year for him was probably overdoing it. To her credit, Phyllis, who had a chatty, high-pitched voice and a birdlike quality, was really quite lovely and evolved. She didn't try to take the place of my mom and was very clear she only wanted to be our friend. That said, I wasn't interested in being part of the *adult* Brady Bunch. Integrating the two families, each with two kids and eventual spouses, wasn't exactly a breeze. For the most part, family holidays proved to be somewhat morose with a motley crew of people who, while very nice, had little in common other than by marriage. (Thank heaven Phyllis made a good brisket, so

I could at least have something to look forward to.) There were enough hurt feelings through weddings, births, and the jockeying for position (in terms of attention) to leave a sour taste in my mouth, but most likely it was just mourning Mom. No matter how old you are, you're always somebody's kid.

My father, in typical Alterna-Dad fashion, considered Phyllis's kids' children his grandchildren, and his excitement and devotion was admirable yet difficult at a time when Dana and I were having a bit of trouble conceiving, and my sister, Susan, had to live through a painful broken engagement only weeks before the wedding (yo, asshole!). Dana still has Susan's wedding dress stashed in one of our closets. Holidays simply weren't easy or pleasant, and Dana and I started doing what anyone else would have done given the circumstances who had *mileage*. We tried to avoid holidays by booking vacations. "Thanksgiving?" "Oops! No can do! We're off to Jamaica for a long weekend, but we'll celebrate the day before . . . ," etc.

Despite the family complications, I did enjoy speaking with Phyllis and found myself calling her now and again for advice. She was very intelligent and compassionate, and always gave me food for thought. Like Marilyn (a.k.a. Maude), she had a way of being both honest and provocative in her thinking. When Dana became pregnant with our twins, Talia and Lucas, we were suddenly confronted with the reality of the situation: What would we and the kids call Phyllis? Nana Phyllis? Grandma? Phyllis? It was a defining point in our relationship and the naming (and/ or branding) really forced us to sit up and take notice. I became obsessed with it, as the name was much like a product carrying strategic underpinnings. After a couple of expensive therapy sessions, Dana and I drove out to Great Neck where Dad was now living in Phyllis's Tudor-style home (but paying the mortgage). We sat down and said, "Now, Phyllis, as you know the twins will be here fairly soon, and we wanted to know what you wanted to be called. Nana? Grandma? Phyllis?" Without missing a beat, Phyllis said, "I'd love to be called Grandma. I want to be grandmother to the children, if that's OK with you?" I wasn't anticipating her immediate reaction, and it took me back initially. But once Phyllis uttered the words, she *was* the spiritual grandmother, and our relationship soon went to a whole new level.

Saying it and being it has always been one of the cornerstones in the ad business as well. If a business takes a corporate strategic intent oath or a pledge without delivering on it, you (the agency) can become toast along with them. If you make a pledge to consumers, you need to deliver on it. This is a critical function and philosophy that extends beyond being honest, knowing who you are, and having integrity. Those qualities are critical to success both personally and professionally—and having them, you have to deliver on the promises you make. You must love who you are, be who you are, and do what you say you can do. If you're the best in any given field, *be* it, don't just say it. If it's difficult, you should still strive to attain it. I've always felt that one shouldn't make promises if he or she can't deliver on them, After all, your creativity and your reputation will eventually pay the price.

A great example of this occurred when Quaker Oats bought Snapple. They quickly moved the headquarters of the brand to Chicago rather than keeping it in Valley Stream, despite many protestations. In addition, they immediately wanted a new campaign. While we were proud of the successful letters campaign we, as still a fairly young company who wanted to keep the business, obliged them by going into creative development for another campaign. After rigorous testing, a young and talented team of (now well-known directors) Mike Maguire and Tom Kuntz, came up with a wonderful new campaign called "We want to be number three." It followed the strategy we had created: "100 percent natural." We felt that an honest, no-nonsense corporate statement would be breakthrough. The idea being that Snapple wasn't competing with Coke or Pepsi in the cola wars but was happy to be who they were, and that a number-three position was valued. We shot a fabulous commercial directed by Spike Lee, which was filmed as a parade for the brand with flags waving and twirlers with a crooner belting out "We want to be number three," all to the song "Born Free." The campaign and insight were truly hysterical and consumers really responded as they saw Snapple as an outsider brand that didn't conform and do things the way everyone else did. Most people in the United States are conditioned to want to be number one or at least number two, but number three? Snapple, which was always a quirky brand (we were explicitly told by Quaker Oats *not* to use the word *quirky*), was ready to commit to this positioning and being number three to Coke and Pepsi could have been incredibly lucrative. A step away from our letters campaign, yes, but a bold positioning and strategy, nonetheless. In the end, Quaker Oats ran a short flight of the spots but pulled it before it really had a chance to run. I'm not sure why, but maybe they thought being number three was un-American, we joked. Or maybe just not Quaker Oats! I'm not sure I ever got the feeling they were particularly interested in Snapple being the brand it actually was when they bought it (and that, my friends, is an opinion). The fantastic brand we had helped build into a phenomenon was its own *quirky* (yeah) thing. They seemed to take the strategy and the branding for granted. In the end, trying to pasteurize Snapple took away its honesty, its integrity, and confused its identity. Then they lost a fortune. And we lost the account, which in some ways was a relief. I remember the day we lost the business that the sky opened up and there was a huge thunderstorm. How fitting! At the end of the day, Snapple was a unique, bold brand, and making a bold statement and claim is always a wonderful thing if you can and are willing to back it up!

*   *   *   *

After Phyllis uttered the words *I want to be the grandmother,* she already was, and she became a great one, always taking out photos of all the kids and displaying them equally. A few short years later, when Phyllis became ill in the final stages of breast cancer, she and Dana would talk for hours on the phone. And one night, she told Dana, "I'm scared." Dana said, "Phyllis, you're not going anywhere. You have to meet the new baby." (Dana was pregnant again with our third child), and she and Phyllis shared a special bond over the new baby's arrival. After Dana gave birth, she immediately took Georgia Rose, as promised, out to Great Neck to introduce her to Phyllis. Phyllis was frail, and Dana placed Georgia Rose in Phyllis's arms so she could hold and feed her, even though she was hardly strong enough to lift her. The photos of Phyllis in her turban kissing her granddaughter, Georgia Rose, are amazing and moving.

Sadly, Phyllis passed away soon after Dana and Georgia Rose's visit. Dana and I truly miss Phyllis and talk about her all the time. Stanley Ira always said he was lucky in love and married two wonderful women, and he did. He was also never shy to talk about my mom in front of Phyllis and called her his first sweetheart, and he called Phyllis his young buck. My father (or was it Woody Allen?) always said the heart is a wonderful muscle when it comes to love, you just need to exercise it. A great lesson. Funny that just when Dana and I *truly* fell in love with Phyllis, she died. The old saying is true, you really don't know what you have until it's gone.

*   *   *   *

This philosophy, among a few others that burnish over time, remind me of experiences I've had while in Capri, where I've vacationed during the summers for nearly thirty-five years, since my teen tour (thanks to Alterna-Dad and Marilyn). For some reason, I have always been drawn to this incredibly scenic and glamorous island off the coast of Naples, feeling a special connection. The only word for Capri is *magical*. It magically has the best of everything. The best views. The best food. The best shopping. The best weather. The best architecture. Quite simply, it doesn't get any better, and I've tried to go as often as I can, which isn't often enough. After going there most of my adult life, I've gotten to know many people on the island. And when last I returned, a store owner, whom I've known for many years, kissed me on both cheeks and gave me the ultimate compliment (or so she thought), "You've been coming so long, you're *almost a caprese!*" Clearly, I'm not Italian; I only speak *menu*, and I don't own a home there. But for me, whether or not I'm a bona fide *caprese,* Capri is a state of mind; it's what we know in the ad business as psychographics, not demographics.

I have also learned a great lesson in branding from local businesses, who don't necessarily have all the state-of-the-art resources that someone in let's say in New York might have. A number of years back, I met one of the great characters in Capri, Franco from the Villa Verde Restaurant. My dear friend Bippy Siegel's parents, the late great Richard and his wonderful wife, Gail, introduced us. They were always in residence at the Grand Hotel Quisisana.

Dana and I on the steps of the Grand Hotel Quisisana

They were very friendly with Franco, who always took great care of them (and us) at the restaurant, which occupies a prime garden location in the center of Capri.

Franco was a legend at Villa Verde (and on the island), not only because of his great, big, warm personality and twinkle in his eye, but as Mrs. Siegel would always say, "He's just fun. And the food tastes better!" When Dana and I brought the twins for dinner, Franco would come over, and the conversation would go something like this: "Tonight I have fresh tomatoes from Franco's garden" (and he'd hold up a lush ripe tomato fresh from the vine). "I have chicken from Franco's farm" (the chicken would be brought out on a silver platter for a viewing). "I have a rocket salad and fresh mozzarella from Franco's cows. I have fresh fish Franco caught off the Faraglioni" (the fish would almost swim to the table). The kids would giggle at Franco's antics. When we ordered a pizza, Franco would bring a pie in the shape of a heart for Dana or the girls. And when he served a dish, he would always place the dish in front of the guest, and with flourish and gusto say, "From Franco with love. *Amore!*" Franco was as big a character as Brandpa, and equally opinionated. "*Don't* have that tonight, have *this*. It's fresh from Franco's garden, with love." Franco would take my son, Lucas, into the kitchen to show him "Franco's fresh pasta." He would regale us with stories about what Mariah Carey ordered from him. Franco made no bones about wanting big tips and would delight in getting a fifty-euro bill, which he would flash to his comrades. All the young waiters loved, adored, and respected Franco, and what he said went. The last night of the trip, we were always given personalized black T-shirts with white letters that said "Franco with Love." And back in New York, we got Christmas cards from Franco and the Villa Verde staff. I was always so impressed that Franco remembered every customer, or pretended to. Franco was the Frank Sinatra of restaurant owners. Or so I thought.

Three summers ago, we went back to Capri and Franco was no longer there. He had become ill with cancer. When we inquired, we found out a lot more about Franco, his family, and where he lived. We had always just assumed that Franco owned the restaurant. Not that it mattered, but we just thought that Franco was the owner because of his larger-than-life presence, his marketing skills, and the fact that he just conveyed that it was his business. It turned out that Franco did not own Villa Verde, but was the most incredible waiter and general manager. It is a great lesson to everyone everywhere that *whatever* you do, be the best at it, and he was. Truthfully, Franco's shtick and branding was up there with the best of them. I could have put Franco in a room with Martha Stewart, and I guarantee she would have been enthralled.

Today, whether it's the open air taxi driver who advertises on the side of his taxi, or my friends serving the best veal Milanese at the superb Al Grottino, Capri is, and always will be, the most magical of places. The next generation has learned from the best.

BRAND EXTENSION

CHAPTER FIFTEEN
INNOVATION TASTES GREAT

THE NEXT GENERATION IS, OF course, on all of our minds regarding the future of our industries. In order to look to the future, one must also take stock of the past. When I first met Kenneth Cole, I remember I looked at all those white shoe boxes he had lying around his office and all his blank white shopping bags and told him I thought they could be ads as well. He agreed, and we did a lot of design work and branding work for what we considered a real new medium. It was a new way to use clients' assets. It was innovative. It was integral. Innovation has always been something impor-tant to kbp and to me person-ally. We have always been in search of the new and differ-ent, but not just for difference's sake; it had to make sense. People always chuckle when we say we invented street-stenciling for Bamboo Lingerie: "From here it looks like you could use some new underwear," signed Bamboo Lingerie on the con-verted sidewalk. (The copycats didn't think to use washable paint and were arrested for defacing public property.)

How about a thong?

Or that kbp's LIME unit and Claudia Strauss invented the pop-up store for Target and Delta Song for people to experience the brands in a totally new way: sitting in the new airplane seats and eating their food as if at street level in a retail space. Or advertising on fruit for Snapple. We found a way to put thousands of stickers on real mangoes for the launch of Mango Madness: the stickers looking like the Chiquita Banana sticker reading "now available in Snapple" in the grocery aisles. We were one of the first to do a content deal, for our client Meow Mix, creating a TV show called *Meow TV,* the first TV show for *cats* that Oxygen bought as a real show, not just as paid advertising. The show, which was actually created to entertain our feline friends, even made Jay Leno's monologue and virtually every news station in the country.

Innovation in marketing can be serious or have a sense of humor, but *you* have to be *first* to create real attention. In 1988, in the early years of the agency, Jon and I published our first book, called *Under the Radar.* Although we were very young, it was excerpted in most industry trades and was on prescribed reading lists in college courses before you could say "Hennessy martini" (which we also invented). We also realized, after the fact, that the book was a blueprint and set a whole copycat industry in motion, with other agencies adopting an integrated platform and doing under-the-radar or 360-degree work. Suddenly, it became *the* industry standard. I wish I had a dime for every small agency that popped up saying they were doing "under-the-radar " or "360-degree" work, like ads on fruit, in urinals, or on the sidewalk. While imitation is the greatest form of flattery, it can also be incredibly annoying. Recently, the *Wall Street Journal* ran an article on street-stenciling and only said it had been invented in the eighties (like big shoulder pads and high hair) without giving us credit. (Annoying.) It can also spark direct competition, which is not necessarily a bad thing as it keeps you moving ahead creatively.

Another form of innovation—technological innovation—will always lead to marketing innovation. After all, you can't create the next great iPad app unless you already have the iPad. That said, I recently tweeted this: "The medium may be the message, but the message is still the message." (I tweet an ad every day called Ad of the Day. Follow me!) Just because the film industry has video/DVD stores doesn't mean it doesn't still need to make great movies. And just because the medium is moving from TV to digital doesn't mean you still don't need big fresh campaign ideas and great branding ideas on YouTube!

The one thing that technology has changed, though, is *the way* people communicate. It is no longer just paid brand ads talking *to* people, but people taking control of the brands. In addition, the phrase *fast, good, and cheap* is how people want it and need it, and we need to be able to hand the brands over to them. When people ask me if technology will bring an end to the ad industry, I don't think it's the end of marketing or advertising. I do however think it has heralded the end of the traditional "brand campaign," though. Companies today cannot really afford, nor should they, multimillion-dollar brand campaigns. Only the largest companies can afford the investment of a multimillion-dollar spend on the Super Bowl or in the mass market. Technology has leveled the playing field and that's a good thing.

I had lunch last year with the well-known CEO of a company widely considered one of the best and purest players in digital marketing. We both agreed that agencies like his are moving toward brand, and agencies like ours are moving toward digital, and one day soon, we'll end up in the same place. The only difference is the traditional agencies still get paid (horror of all horrors!) higher fees. I jokingly said to him, "You make smart cars. We make smart cars, too. But we're also making the horse and buggy (TV ads)—and we're making the *Rolls-Royce* of horse and buggies. So I'll take the next five years, no prob!"

One of the real benefits of working for so many clients is getting a window into a multitude of organizations, their corporate cultures and levels of cultural innovation. Small clients or small family-owned businesses are always quirky and unique, and are often a mirror of the family culture. When it comes to business innovation, I have always been fascinated that there are generally three categories that businesses usually fall into. They are: 1) companies that are fixed in their culture and way of doing business and their conservative ideals, and feel they have no need to change or innovate; 2) companies that are fixed in their culture and way of doing business but *say* or pay lip service to change and innovation but hardly do; and 3) innovative companies that live and breathe innovation in every pore. Apple is one such company. From every product, to the retail and in-store experience to the visionary way products, marketing, and design integrate, Steve Jobs doesn't just say it, he actually *is* it. In general, since not every agency can work with Apple, I actually respect both companies at either end of the spectrum more than the second option (in the middle). The innovative company (the third option) will always be my favorite, but I do get a special kick out of certain companies who are just honest about who they are. Why? Well the companies that just pay lip service to innovation tire out the creative department and spin everyone's wheels, as they'll never buy real innovation. On our side of the business, most agencies say they are innovative or at least want to believe it. It's like an accountant saying he's conservative. They all say they are, but like my old accountant Ken Starr, just because they all say it doesn't mean they are.

Innovation is the adman's point of entry. But if you're an adman who hasn't pushed the needle, invented anything, tried to sell something fresh or new, or seen something from a completely new angle, then you're not at the forefront and hopefully staying ahead of the game. You're going to be hanging on, trying to stay *in* the game.

This summer, Dana and I took a second honeymoon in France without the kids. We hadn't been in many years, and we drove seven hours to eat and sleep at the famed L'Oustau de Baumanière in Les Baux de Provence. The sixteenth-century inn, which is in a remote corner of Provence, is one of the few places that retains an authentic French quality. That translates to chic, stick-thin French people in couture, smoking like chimneys, and feeding scraps to their dogs under the table. The kitchen, which is widely considered one of the best in France and run under the esteemed chef Jean-André Charial, served one of the most innovative deserts I have ever had, not to mention utterly delicious. It was a crepe, stuffed with a soufflé. Let me repeat that, a *crepe*, stuffed with a *soufflé*. Leave it to the French to think of and then to engineer such a gastronomic feat. But there it was before my eyes and the soufflé hadn't fallen by the time it was stuffed, served, and ready to be eaten.

If you can't be innovative in advertising, you're either a crepe *or* a souf-flé, something that everyone likes that's already *on* the menu. But if you can advertise on fruit or create a TV show that a four-legged animal might watch or invent a new retail experience, then you're the soufflé inside the crepe—sweet, frothy, distinct, and new. And every bite is worth the trip.

*   *   *   *

From the early days of the agency, we thought long and hard of what the integrated agency of the moment would eventually look like well before people in the industry were even thinking about it. Jon and Rosemarie, to their credit, spent a lot of time looking at things like process and even the efficiency of communication through seating plans in order to get disparate groups talking and interacting with one another. We also knew we needed new areas of discipline in the agency that did not exist. So, in 2000, Jon went on to form the media division with a former kbp employee, Barry Lowenthal. It is called the Media Kitchen and is an incredibly suc-cessful entrepreneurial media-planning unit. I decided to form a new unit called Dotglu, which was one of the first digital and direct-mail compa-nies. The digital area wasn't exactly my area of expertise, but I knew enough to know we needed a digital marketing play and that the metrics of acquisition and retention were similar in both the digital and direct areas. I recruited a Thompson alum, Steve Thibodeau, to join and build Dotglu after a bumpy, expensive start. Today, Dotglu is thriving with major companies on its roster such as BMW of North America.

The one thing I have always believed in is something Marilyn (a.k.a. Maude) always said, "The only thing you can count on is change." And I have adopted and tried to live by this adage. After all, if the world is changing around you and all you do is keep your head in the sand, you'll just end up with a mouthful of, well, sand. Since the agency and the busi-ness were growing both horizontally and vertically, we started to get approached by holding companies that were interested in acquiring the agency and its billings. For many years, Jon and I resisted the offers to sell, but we had quite a few meetings with the usual suspects like Sir Martin Sorrell, who tried to acquire us (I asked him if he had fun!), and the Interpublic Group. Jon would always set up these lunches or dinners, and he would say, "Just go and *try* and be nice, OK?" The only time I wasn't was when Jon set up a meeting with a digital private equity guy (during the *first* Internet bubble) who, besides putting his hand on my knee a few times during lunch, actually said that Jon and I should just "give up our business and come work for him since the ad industry was finished." His Harvard acolytes, who were with him, nodded.

I said, "So you think it's wise for us to just up and leave a company with millions in billings and over seventy-five employees [at the time]?"

"Yes, that's what I think, just leave. Come work for me."

"And what would we get?" I asked as I swatted his hand off my knee under the table.

"Oh, we'd see after you're with us a year. Maybe you'd be eligible for some of our stock." (Now defunct.)

I promptly got up and said, "If you all want to stay and continue this charade of a lunch, fine. But I have real work to do back at the office," and stormed out.

Every year one of my great mentors, Jerry Della Femina, and his wife, Judy, host a Fourth of July party at their stunning East Hamptons oceanside manse. No one is more gracious, lovely, and a better host and hostess than Jerry and Judy. When Dana and I bought our house in the Hamptons, we reciprocated and had Jerry and Judy over for a small dinner party, and I asked Jerry his thoughts, at the time, about us selling our agency (to a real holding company). Jerry patted me on the back and said, "Of course, you should sell. Why, I've sold my company three times . . . once when I didn't even own it!" We all had a good laugh, but I got the message. Not too long after, I was having lunch with Donny Deutsch, debating our integrated structures, when he told me he'd gotten an incredible offer to sell his agency for a life-changing number. It was too good to be true. And while he had mixed emotions, Donny sold his agency (which had been on a new-business tear for years) to the Interpublic Group in what I would always refer to as "the last *great* deal." Donny looks back today at the sale, and his timing couldn't have been more impeccable.

I've known many ad people who've lived and done well on their wits and timing. Very often, when you're dealing with different accounts across various categories, you become quite good at trending, just by listening to your little voice. In fact, one of our great visionary clients, John Pellegrene, from Target, hired the agency (since he lived in Minneapolis) to give him a monthly trend report. I personally worked on these and they ranged from shopping the latest trends to predictive reports ranging from "the popularity of the pod shape" to "trends in pet habits," which helped keep John and Target in tune with what was happening in New York and Europe. I mention this because when you are the beneficiary of trend information, you can be ahead of the game in decision-making as well. And with that info John used our proximity and eye to the greatest effect, helping to increasing Target's billings.

Early the spring of 2005, our friend George Fertitta called us and said he wanted to introduce us to Miles Nadal, who owned a smaller but influential advertising holding company, MDC Partners. George had sold his agency, Margeotes/Fertitta + Partners, to them and encouraged us to meet with Miles. We took the meeting and found Miles both energetic, engaging, and visionary. (Miles's forward vision and leadership, especially in the digital space, has, in only a few short years, propelled MDC to its position as one of the most sought after holding companies.) Hearing Jerry's words resonate in the back of my head, I remember walking into Jon's office and plopping myself down on his sofa. "Jon, I think we should consider selling." Jon was feeling the same way. We generally have always been in agreement (within a 10 to 20 percent range), and when MDC became a serious suitor, we hired veteran deal maker/accountant/heavyweight David Wiener to negotiate for us.

I have always believed: 1) that ad agencies are either three years ahead or behind their reputations, and 2) that major shifts occur in a biblical seven-year cycle. The economy had been at its frothiest, and we wouldn't know what the economy would be like in six or seven years (hello!). When we crafted our deal, obviously, we had no idea just how fortuitous the timing would be. Unlike Jerry, I'm not sure Jon and I will be able to sell the agency again (when we don't own it), but selling on the eve of the great recession wasn't too bad a decision, either. I also believe that MDC received a great moneymaking asset with years of goodwill attached to the name, so it was *very* nice all the way around. That said, when you sell an asset or something you've lovingly grown for almost a quarter of a century, it can take a bit of an emotional toll. I was lucky that I had a few friends who sold businesses. And they gave me great advice, "If you sell the agency, either be prepared to change your role—or to leave." I took that to heart and decided to stay as chairman, which I think has been a great role for me because I enjoy being a coach and having a bit more time to invent new ideas and products.

Whether it's seeing a white shoe box and seeing an ad or branding on it, seeing the trends in doggie couture or looking at market dips and peaks, sometimes as an ad guy you see things other people don't. And if you see that the times are changing, there's a good chance you'll have a sense of timing as well. I also believe the average person can do this, too, if they read enough information (readily available on the Web) and ask the right questions of the right mentors. All in all, if you look at the bigger picture, you might end up having a real one on your wall. As I always quote my dad, "No one ever went broke taking a profit." I couldn't agree more, especially when consumer data dictates that most people do the opposite of what they should, i.e., they buy high and sell low as opposed to buying low and selling high. Look at commodity prices. Now that they've peaked, the herd stampedes to buy commodities. Not that owning commodoties is a bad idea, but bubbles suck people in like a wave and then crash over them—when they least expect it. It's all about timing.

Advertising is a business that's all about timing as well, and if you don't believe it, all you have to do is tune in to the Super Bowl. Spots regularly play off celebrities du jour or current political or economic forecasts, or what I call the song or the gimmick of the moment. Also, the bigger the client, the more of these shticks they will try and load into *one* commercial. Animals, celebrities, hit songs, animation, boobs, whatever it takes. It's all about being all current and taking advantage of *all* trends. That's one sort of timing. And it incorporates the fact that advertising is also about change as it relates to timing. That's being current. As my wise mother, Marilyn (a.k.a. Maude), always said, "Change is the one thing in life you can count on."

194

ALMOST, ALMOST FAMOUS

I learned another great lesson about timing (a bird in the hand is worth two in the bush) when I was just starting out. And it was a good kick in the teeth to boot. When I was in my early thirties, I wrote a very funny play called *Dying to Meet You*. It was a post-suburban comedy in which spirits come back from the afterlife to comment on the living. As I was on the board of David Mamet's Atlantic Theater Company, my friend Neil Pepe (who is now a well-respected director) helped me with a reading or two. While it wasn't right for the Atlantic, Neil encouraged me and I sent it to the Jewish Repertory Theater in New York, which first produced wonderful plays such as *Driving Miss Daisy*. (It was glamorously housed in a basement below a deli or supermarket.) I received word that the artistic director wanted to do the play for their fall 1991 season. I couldn't have been more thrilled. This, of course, was all extracurricular to running the agency, so it's not as if it was a full-time job or that I was living a life in the theater. One day after work, I went down to the theater to meet the director they had assigned me. He was, as I recall, fairly young and arrogant, and I didn't gel with his vision of the play. Not understanding the theater, the season, or the timing, I asked if I could find my own director of choice, and the artistic director just shrugged and said, "If that's what you want." After a long intensive search, I sent the play to a well-known comedic director. After two weeks, he called me and said, "I love your play. It's very funny."

"And?"

"And I'd love to do it."

"That's great!"

"But I can't."

"Why not?" I said, crestfallen.

"Because I just finished a play on Broadway that also had dead characters, and while it's completely different, I don't want to be associated with two shows that have a similar creative device." Needless to say I was less than happy.

A few weeks later, my agent sent the play to none other than the distinguished actor/director Tony Roberts, of Woody Allen fame. Tony read the play and thought it was very funny and agreed to direct it. Everyone was thrilled, and the first reading he did was star-studded, featuring well-known actors like Jessica Walter, Anne Meara, and Kristen Johnston. I invited family and friends to the reading, and even though the play needed work, it was an incredible experience to hear such fine actors read my words on a real stage. Soon after, Tony called me and said, "Richard, I have some good news and bad news. The good news is that I think the play is hilarious; as funny as anything Woody has written, but I just got the opportunity to take over the lead in *Victor/Victoria*, and I am going to do it. So the bad news is I cannot direct your play." Of course, I was even more crestfallen, and the next day I called the artistic director of the Jewish Repertory Theater to tell him I needed to find another director. He promptly told me that as much as he wanted to wait for me, I'd now missed the fall season. He left after that season, and *Dying to Meet You* is still at the bottom of my desk drawer.

Looking back, I realize I made a huge mistake. I didn't take the director they offered me, and I didn't say, "Thank you, this is an amazing opportunity." Likewise, sometimes, the agency has pitched for a piece of business, and while not getting the lead account or coming in first, we did such a good job, we were awarded a smaller brand or a different part of the integrated business. I have often used the term *account karma* to describe either getting or not getting a piece of business. A few years back, the agency was included in a pitch for BMW. Car accounts have long been considered the Holy Grail of the ad business. Our dear friend and industry legend Carl Ally called them a "transportation thing with wheels" and urged us to get one. A car account was not only prestigious and lucrative, but validating. Donny Deutsch had always dreamed of a big national car account (bigger than local dealers), and he had spent a great deal of time, energy, and money pitching numerous car accounts before winning Mitsubishi and becoming Agency of the Year. We'd come close on Jaguar and Hyundai in long, expensive, painful pitches. BMW, however, was the biggest prize. We spent an enormous amount of time, energy, and money not only on the pitch but also on the rehearsals. It's not untrue that one must have great ideas but also the theatrical skills to sell them. We created and orated new campaigns, made videos, and created the most gorgeous full-size brand book covered in driving glove leather. I remember walking with Jon around BMW's corporate parking lot right before the pitch, feeling we were in our prime, but also feeling so nervous about presenting. No matter how experienced you are, speaking in front of an organization of twenty to fifty people can be very daunting when the stakes are so high. Our team did an outstanding job, and after we gave it our all, the waiting period was—and often is—difficult and torturous.

I was in the office when Jon got the call. I saw the crestfallen look on his face and knew we didn't get it. However, they were so impressed with Steve Thibodeau and our digital offering at Dotglu that they told us we were going to get a smaller part of the business. It was difficult to hear that we weren't getting the big TV portion of the business, and the interactive and direct part seemed nice—yet, at first, like a side dish, not the main course. Seven years later, the digital portion of BMW, run through Dotglu, is one of the most valuable calling cards for kbp. The agency they hired to do the TV commercials is no longer around, and we just completed two Super Bowl commercials, our first! Hard work, dedication, and timing helped us win in the long term, when initially we thought we'd lost.

I've seen competitors get angry and throw things at the TV when they lose a pitch. I've seen grown men and women go on drinking binges and try to throw their colleagues under the bus when things don't go their way. Perhaps they don't know how to turn lemons into lemonade, but after twenty-four years, I put it down to seizing the opportunity and embracing the cards in the deck. And then playing your best hand. Sometimes, just sometimes, a loser can come up a winner. And sometimes the account just isn't meant for you! Also, sometimes in the advertising business, the timing and outcome are not entirely always within your control. Sometimes you do your best work and lose the account. Sometimes you do mediocre or fair work and get more business. The trick is to understand timing. To take what you can get when you can get it, appreciate it, and do a great job. Because sometimes when you try to over-direct things, sometimes, just sometimes, you end up without a director.

CHAPTER 16
WHEN YOU HAVE A GREAT IDEA—
BOTTLE IT!

WHEN ADMEN SELL THEIR AGENCIES, it does not mean they don't stay in the business, as in my case I've stayed on as chairman of Kirshenbaum Bond Senecal + Partners. When Donny Deutsch transformed himself from adman to TV host, I questioned my own entertainment aspirations and came back empty-handed. Being a TV celebrity was really not my goal, although I was asked by Plum TV founder Tom Scott to host a fun interview show for the channel called *Creative Lunch*. For a season, I interviewed interesting creative people such as Cynthia Rowley, Morgan Spurlock, and Mort Zuckerman over real meals (again the food!). Donny had me on his show, *The Big Idea,* a few times, which was both fun and flattering. But many times, when I get the call to do a short segment for the CBS *Early Show,* on CNBC as an industry talking head, or giving an occasional opinion on *really* important matters like Britney's or Paris's newest ad deals (*yawn*) I find a way to worm out of it, unless it's a really big segment for the Super Bowl (often I report on the ads for the *New York Post* and TV stations) or something else of equal interest (to me).

Three years ago, I was given a different kind of commercial opportunity. I'd been introduced to Janice Min, who was, at the time, editor of *Us Weekly,* by my public relations consultant Sean Cassidy (*not* the 1970s icon) who is president of DKC Public Relations. Sean and Janice thought it would be a good idea for me to become a member of their Fashion Police since I was both interested in fashion and could write a mean one-liner. I thought it would be fun but had to convince Dana because she felt it wasn't serious enough for me. After all, what was a male ad agency owner doing commenting on female celebrity clothing? What would the dads at school think? I thought of the Little League coaches who spurned me and said, "That's just the point," and immediately agreed to do it.

At first, many of my one-liners were rejected as being *too* risqué, like the time I wrote about Oscar-winner Marcia Gay Harden's gown, "I'm not getting a *hard-on* over this dress." But I eventually got the hang of it and enjoyed having my postage-size photo and quips published in a national magazine. Suddenly, I went from being just an ad guy to also being a fashion maven. Clients called and awarded us business and sold me through to their organization as a fashionista. A major Academy Award–winning actress (a client) asked her people to tell my people to stop writing about her. Private school mothers asked me if I gave their couture a thumbs-up at school events. Finally, *Us Weekly* named me one of its top twenty-five most stylish New Yorkers. I soon found myself on the red carpet and in the VIP room with Mayor Bloomberg, Dylan Lauren, and get this, backstage with Tori (Spelling) and Dean (McDermott)! I was stopped in airports, and it also led me to being featured in the *Financial Times* World News profile for my style (pocket squares, cufflinks, and Italian suits). I made runner-up for various best-dressed lists and started getting photographed at galas. I've finished my Fashion Police tour of duty, and this little bit of frivolous fun showed me that a little bit of fun goes a long way, and you never know what you can expect when you put yourself out there. So what if the fathers at the hockey rink asked me to redesign the uniform (it's true!).

Actually, developing new products—not just branding and marketing those of others—is something that interests me. It's a new and exciting venture, and I've done this with a fabulous new product I helped to invent and its legendary namesake.

Many years ago, Dana and I fell upon Jamaica. Strangely, its rocky emerald caves reminded us a bit of Capri, and we instantly fell in love, returning to Jamaica regularly. Luckily for me, one of my closet friends, Jordan Schur, loved Jamaica, too. And since he was president of Geffen Records, at the time, he had gotten friendly with legendary Island

Records founder Chris Blackwell, who owns the incredibly glamorous GoldenEye Hotel & Resort, among others. Jordan rented out the entire resort for his wedding, which proved to have more than one love affair, leading me to discovering another Jamaican treasure at the wedding. I got to spend some time chatting and getting to know Chris Blackwell. He gave me a wonderful tour of GoldenEye (the former home of Ian Fleming who wrote every Bond novel there). I instantly fell in love with GoldenEye and with Chris's cool and relaxed creative demeanor.

One of the things I've learned over the years is that people who are often the most inventive and innovative actually spend less time when it comes to looking at some of their own assets within their brand portfolio. This can even be true of people who are legendary regarding how people perceive them. Chris was intrigued with my marketing background and asked me what I thought of GoldenEye. I thought it was and is an incredible marketing opportunity, but looking at Chris in an objective way, I asked him if he'd ever done anything with his own brand: his name, Blackwell. Now one has to understand that in Jamaica, Chris is often likened to Warren Buffet. He discovered Bob Marley, founded Island Records, and brought reggae to the world. Not to mention a few other *small* acts like U2. Having stayed at the Round Hill Hotel and Villas (one of the nicest and most pedigreed on the island), I had seen how much the Jamaican people appreciated Ralph Lauren (who bought Bill and the iconic Babe Paley's villa and helped bring back luster to the resort). It came to my attention that Jamaica wanted to put Ralph on an actual postage stamp, as well as Chris. I took a page from Ralph and said to Chris, "If you ever want to do something in your name, let me know."

We continued our correspondence and friendship over many trips to the island. The next year, I was back in Jamaica and called Chris and threw the idea at him of doing a Jamaican coffee or water line, thinking the Blackwell name would work very well for that. Chris shrugged and turned me down; it wasn't something he was passionate about. He is also very modest and wasn't convinced he wanted to lend his actual name to a product. Then a few months later, on another trip for spring break, I saw the obvious. I'd been friendly with a bartender at Half Moon (another stunning villa resort we stayed at for years with the kids), and he gave me a new drink called a Governor's House, with a black rum floater. The dark rum stayed on top of the delicious papaya mixture. That very day, I called Chris and asked him if he liked the idea of a dark gold rum—called Blackwell. "Yes, I do," he said evenly. "In fact, my grandfather and his brother used to own J. Wray and Nephew (which is one of the finest rum producers in the Caribbean), and when I was younger, I was meant to take over the business." Little did I know that three years later, I'd be back in Jamaica, launching Blackwell Fine Jamaican Rum and having the prime minister toast it at the event, as well as invite us to the Jamaican White House for breakfast.

By looking at Chris's Jamaican portfolio and equities, I saw something that was there to bring to the surface: his incredible career and lifestyle and Jamaica's finest black gold rum as well as his good name. Building the brand has been a labor of love. I've gotten to work side by side with one of the most interesting creative entrepreneurs, and within the month, we will be bringing Blackwell Fine Jamaican Rum to the United States through our new American distributor, Domaine Select. Sometimes you don't need to look outside, but inside, to find the gold. It's all a matter of vision and taste.

Looking inside always gives you a good view of your own ethics, as well. Have you behaved and produced in ways that you can be proud of? One of the most interesting things about working with Chris was that when someone puts their name on something you cannot settle unless it's the very, very best. We spent the right amount of time to get the label and liquid just right, as we have felt Jamaica needed a true luxury product it could be proud of. And now that it is we feel great to share it with the Jamaican and U.S. markets. Sometimes one idea spurs another. Last year, during the summer, I was having dinner with one of my closest friends, David Mitchell, in the city (our wives live out at the beach, giving us the distinction of being what I laughingly refer to as *Desperate Husbands*). I was showing David the bottle of the rum, since I had it in my bag, and got into a discussion about branding. I was mentioning the idea that people can become brands with the right association and level of integrity. That weekend we both attended a wedding, and sat next to each other. When it came time for the groom to kiss the bride, I quipped, "Well this would be a perfect branding opportunity for the rabbi to slip the groom a Rabbi Mintz Kosher Mints," since the rabbi who was officiating was named Rabbi Mintz. David turned to me and said, "That's very funny but may be serious business." After a bit of digging and some research, we concluded there are virtually no branded kosher confectionary mints in the marketplace, due to the fact that most mints are made from gelatin, made from non-kosher animals. One year later, we have just launched Rabbi Mints and have received our first thousand samples. Our tagline is "The Chosen Mint," and a portion of the sales will be given to charity. Just this week the *New York Post* ran an article in which comedian Jackie Mason quipped that the new brand was "a mitzvah because the mints will help promote happy relationships . . . [the rabbi] is just lucky his name isn't Rabbi Garlic—or Sewer." Suddenly the mints are flying off the shelves at the rate of 200 tins a week and we got our first online order today!

Whether it's meeting a famed Jamaican entrepreneur and envisioning a black gold rum and bringing it to market or inventing and marketing something that currently doesn't exist in the marketplace, like a kosher mint, seeing new things and trying new things tastes good to me. I'm proud of how and what I've produced, and continue to be, thanks to the values my parents gave me, and look forward to creating more brands. After all, there's nothing tastier to me than the creation of new ideas.

CHAPTER SEVENTEEN
IF IT'S GOING TO HAPPEN, IT'S GOING TO HAPPEN IN NEW YORK

SOMETIMES YOU AREN'T CREATING AND producing campaigns or products that you are proud of. Sometimes when you're an adman, you spend your time helping people and communities in crucial ways that you are very proud to be able to do. It happened in New York.

Over the years, New York has actually become quite safe as real estate prices have outpaced most of the criminal element (unless you count a certain element of Wall Street), but it is still surreal to be sledding in Central Park on a winter's day with the kids, thinking you're "anywhere" and look up and see skyscrapers looming over the trees. And while under Giuliani and Bloomberg New York has become safer, better, and cleaner, it's still New York City and anything can happen. It is actually true that the crime went down because the criminals could no longer *afford* New York and were outsourced to the suburbs. So let it be heard through America: *Hear ye, hear ye. New York City is now safe for Midwesterners. The crack den on Tenth Avenue is now a luxury highrise!* But while everyday life happens in the city, it's also a caffeinated place where everything can happen, and usually does.

I had taken my car downtown on a beautiful morning like any other. I stopped into Starbucks for a caramel macchiato (tall, extra caramel), and I was crossing Sixth Avenue. I heard a surreal inhuman sound and a burning piece of paper fell into my coffee cup, making that sizzle sound. All around me people were looking up. Now in New York *only* the tourists look up. Sort of like no one sees people *walking* in LA and when they do, something's up.

There was a large fiery hole in the World Trade Center. That was surreal to see, but New Yorkers can be more than a bit jaded. Everyone has heard sirens before. People were immobile, though, and I heard a woman say aloud she thought a commuter plane had flown into the building. People just stood there immobilized. I remember it felt like slow motion. Now I know this sounds crazy and it is, but in New York City, you see crazy shit and go on your merry way. You could be having dinner alfresco and someone can get shot in front of you (in the old days), and people call the police and go on eating their dinner. Seeing a famous person is also no biggie. A famous politician—a big yawn. When the president is in town, everyone thinks it's a big pain because of the traffic. I once was jogging around the reservoir, and Bill Clinton came running by with his Secret Service agents, and the runners bitched him out and complained. I say this because the mentality is that nothing is a big deal and essentially you should mind your own business.

After standing around looking at the so-called "commuter plane accident," I went into the office to see what the staff and news was saying about it and to check on a new business meeting that was going on. Within minutes of hearing what the foot powder manufacturer had to say, we were alerted to the second plane hitting the second tower. I excused myself, even though the foot powder manufacturer wanted to know why the meeting was breaking up. "Because we're under attack," my assistant shrieked. I felt weak in the knees as we came to the awful conclusion that our world and our lives had changed in that moment and forever.

Now I wouldn't say we were two blocks away from the towers, but we were certainly in their shadow, and they clearly loomed above us. If they fell *over,* that would have been curtains in our area, out on the streets. We immediately told the staff to either go home or stay inside. I ran outdoors, and the shocking sight was the sky completely full of smoke and papers, which would continue for days afterwards. I got panicked calls from Dana and my father, who both said, "Get the heck out of there and quick." First we tried to take care of the shocked staff, and formulated a plan with the partners. Once our people started to leave, I got into my car and drove uptown. I distinctly remember it feeling like a modern day

Pompeii as the first tower started to collapse and we tried to outpace the debris up Sixth Avenue. I only looked back once, and it was a humbling, shocking sight. White billowing smoke, papers like confetti in the air, and the thought of all those poor people hanging out windows hoping . . . I was sick to my stomach but got uptown as fast as I could to get home to Dana and the babies, who were newborn twins at the time. Once I reached the Upper West Side, I walked through the park to the East Side, where we lived. I'll never forget the eerie silence of all the avenues as masses of people walked and walked, all in shock.

It's hard to describe the horrible smell that engulfed downtown and traveled uptown that evening and for days afterward. After grabbing a quick motionless dinner, I put Dana and the kids in our car and sent them out to our rented cottage in Quogue. Dana begged me to come with them, but I just couldn't leave the shocked staff. It felt like London during the war as I waved to Dana and the kids, hoping they would make it out of the city, which they eventually did. I felt like leaving the city at that time and had a huge pit in my stomach, but thought running away would have been a cowardly act.

The next day, I booked rooms at an uptown private club I belong to in the city and had an agency meeting there for all the senior executives and staff. The club, which is a grand old club, didn't change its policy about allowing jeans, and many of our creative staff wore slacks, jackets, and ties for the first time. This was a bit strange given the circumstances, but the club had a certain standard and I respect that. We spent the day calling clients and reassuring them that everyone was OK (and getting the work in progress out the door), but it felt hollow and terrible and no one knew if there was going to be another attack. Our offices and downtown area were closed off, and we didn't know when they would reopen.

When we were finally allowed back downtown, I felt badly and a bit paranoid about the air quality and was resentful of my friends who had offices uptown. That said, we threw ourselves into organizing babysitting services and raising donations for the firehouse around the corner from our office and for other social services. I had never before seen the sadness, mourning, and lack of innocence that attended 9/11. No one living here in America had. The loss of friends and family and police and firefighters tallied up over the weeks that followed. A sadness that occurred since those awful days has been imprinted in our minds forever. I walk by the downtown firehouses daily with the photos of the young, fallen heroes. It never ceases to be sobering.

Community service and patriotism all came into play in those days, weeks, and months that followed. That gave us all hope; inspiration even. It was encouraging to see downtown regenerate itself that Christmas. In order to help the downtown economy, so badly hurt by the attacks, we made the decision to have our agency holiday party in a restaurant at the tip of Manhattan, near the 9/11 zone. The fact that it had a view of the Statue of Liberty had all the meaning as we celebrated and mourned at the same time. New York would never be the same and neither would we. Dana and I had a lapse of thought only once about moving out of the city with our new twins. Although 9/11 happened and our kids now went to nursery school behind cement barricades and through a metal detector, we only took one trip out of the city to look at houses in the suburbs. In the end, we couldn't face detaching ourselves from the city. It isn't just the city where all the creative people flock to. It remains the city of dreams for all who have thrived living and working here. For us, moving away would have reminded me of leaving the city the day after the attacks. Very often when I travel, people ask me where I'm from, and I say New York. Inevitably they ask where my family is from. When I say New York, they seem perplexed, as if no one is actually *from* New York. Raising your kids in New York isn't easy, yet removing ourselves from such a vibrant, creative city would be harder still.

CHAPTER EIGHTEEN
PASS THE TORCH

ALTERNA-DAD'S LOGIC HAS ALWAYS BEEN to question and not to take anything at face value. Harry Truman has always been one of his heroes, because Harry Truman did one fundamental thing that Stanley Ira loved (and I've been taught to love). As president, he asked everyone's opinion and then came to his own conclusion, unlike some of the other presidents. And that's what I strive for in business, and what I have seen in my most successful clients (like the Steve Wynns of the world).

Stanley Ira once said, "In his day, asking other people their opinion was considered a sign of weakness. But Truman was an unassuming guy from Missouri. He asked people what they thought, then made his own decision, like when he integrated the armed forces in 1948, which not many people talk about." Alterna-Dad enthused, "A very unpopular decision but a major advance in civil rights. Not like these morons today who are for 'don't ask, don't tell.' Gays in the military is the civil rights issue of our time. Someone should take a stand and say they're in—the morons" (given the fact that they're *in* anyway). Of course, that has just recently become the case legally—but Alterna-Dad was talking about this two decades ago. According to Stanley Ira, Truman was the "Sinatra of Presidents"! Thanks to my father, I was brought up understanding the obvious justice of integration, and that has led me to understand the value of a multicultural voice as it applies to business. Marilyn (a.k.a. Maude) was also an integral force in my development. She was strong-willed and strong-minded and made the decision early on to expose me to different people and while it may seem like a small thing, she insisted on sending me to New England during the summers, so I would meet a different group of kids, given the Long Island–centric options.

Summer camp is not exclusively a Jewish rite of passage, but it certainly is a cultural pulse point, especially off the LIE. Very often my WASP friends joked and said, "I don't get this camp thing. What's with Jews and summer camp?" I answered dryly, "Our parents send us away during the summer, but you get shipped off to boarding school all during the year, so ¿qué pasa?"

When it came to summer camp, I'm not sure what possessed them to get it so right, but summers in New Hampshire, away from all the New Yorkers, was sheer genius! New England provided a new species to interact with and the brands were all new to me: Carter overalls, Docksiders, certainly as far as you could get from a Wayne Rogers polyester disco shirt and platforms! Being a New Yorker was somewhat original to the crew from places like Wellesley, Newton, Natick, and Worcester. It also afforded me different social experiences like sailing and windsurfing trips to Maine, or like the time I was thirteen and was invited to a formal by a girl in Worcester. I wore my tan poplin bar mitzvah suit, and within five minutes at the dinner dance dropped a large spoonful of oily mashed potatoes on my crotch, ruining both my suit and my look at the same time. Regardless, getting outside of New York at a young age was interesting. And while I wasn't logging in British Columbia or on the Appalachian Trail, it did me some good. It was also the first time I saw that different places and regions attracted a different brand loyalty. For example, early in my career when we handled the Nathan's Famous account, I had already learned that different regions like different hot dog flavors (i.e., more garlicky in the Northeast and more pork and ballpark oriented in the South). I also saw and heard about institutionalized prejudice, for the first time, where advertisers created the sets of ads for whites and blacks for both the North and the South. As someone who was a child during the civil rights era (and Brandpa's un-PC stereotypes), I was on a different path with my thinking and actions. In college, I integrated my fraternity and was happily introduced to a different sort of fashion and music (it may date me, but the first time I heard rap was when brothers Otis and Tony were spinning in the frat house). In the early eighties, there just wasn't a whole lot of cross-cultural blending going on, as cliché as that may sound.

In business, I am proud to say that under my creative direction, I pushed for and helped bring African American consumers *into* the advertising and stopped advertisers from segregating ads. Certainly this was a vast improvement from the lily-white landscape I inherited in the business. Today, the next step is to encourage multicultural voices to actually *create* the work. Like Alterna-Dad, I haven't been satisfied with the status quo. I've been unhappy that over the years there have been so few African Americans, Latinos, and urban creatives in ad land. If you look at the advertising business, it was an elitist white-shoe business until the 1960s when the first Jews and Italians entered the fray. Next, the baton was passed to women and the industry made great strides. Once we sold our business, the talented and visionary Lori Senecal came on board to become not only President and CEO but one of the first name partners, as in Kirshenbaum Bond Senecal + Partners (and to take the agency into the future). The next frontier is multicultural voices who will hopefully change the way brands communicate. One day, my good friend David Lauren invited me to speak at East Harlem School, which he and his family have been supportive of. I decided to go and speak to the kids. It is a fabulous school with a wonderful group of next-generation superstars. I explained what it was that I did and a girl in pigtails raised her hand and said, "Is that considered work? You can really earn a living doing this?"

What I found out from speaking to all the kids was that they didn't really *know* that there was an industry to go into, or a place they could even earn their living creatively. Once we sold the business, I set out to try and help underserved teens to try and encourage them to enter the ad field. My good friend Alison Fahey, the publisher and editorial director of *AdWeek,* introduced me to Debbie Deutsch and Peter Drakoulias, who started TORCH, a wonderful organization that supports underserved teens through communication and the arts. They immediately helped me construct and implement a scholarship to help mentor and support students. MDC, our parent company, generously provided a matching grant to my own scholarship and now, together, we provide support, funds, internships, and mentorships to young urban creatives who can hopefully enter and change the business with their voices, the way my own voice did. Hopefully, we can pass the torch to a new generation of creative talent.

My dear friend, the late Bob Lessin, who was vice chairman of Jefferies, the esteemed financial institution, was dedicated to a wonderful school on Saint Marks Place called the George Jackson Academy. It is a privately funded school that acts as a private boys' school for the best and brightest young minds, most of whom hail from rough sections of the Bronx and Brooklyn. Bob lectured once a week and told me that out of everything he did, this is what meant the most to him. He asked me to participate in a program where I would mentor and take a few of the boys out to lunch which I did just last week. It was amazing to meet the boys (all dressed in ties and sweaters) and hear them talk about their passion for math, science, and the arts. It was incredibly inspiring, but more inspiring for me!

Getting to know different types of people and having them get to know me will hopefully broaden everyone's point of view. My first Kirshenbaum Scholarship recipient, Camille Crawford, is enrolled at Pace to graduate in '14, is a talented artist, and will start on her internship with us this summer, in addition to all the clients' and friends' kids who currently have the privilege of a summer experience. I think she will learn a great deal but also help teach the other interns what it's like to succeed against the odds.

Hopefully, like Harry, I asked everyone's opinion and then made my own decision. My interest in the industry, giving back, and helping the next generation of voices in the ad business needs to happen and it is my mission to help open the door for underserved teens. Like integrating the armed forces, it's clearly the right thing to do. There was a time when the door was closed to us as well, and sometimes it's not just about inviting people to the party but taking them by the arm and escorting them in. I believe that is what you need to do if you have the privilege of being a good host!

EPILOGUE

I SHOULDN'T HAVE PUT THE sixteen-carat emerald ring in the hummus, but where else was I supposed to hide it? I mean, when you're married to the only Jewish girl in America who threatens to divorce you if you buy her any more jewelry, what would you do? I knew I had to break it to her slowly, so I went into our newly renovated kitchen and arranged a plate of sixteen, pinkie-size carrots: you know, the annoying ones that are dry and tasteless and come in a plastic bag. I arranged them like soldiers on a simple white Crate & Barrel plate and slipped the ring onto the remaining carrot. When suddenly, there she was.

"What are you making?"

"Oh nothing, just some carrots and hummus," I said as I shoved the ring back into the hummus container and covered it quickly with the plastic lid.

There are many big stones that come with names, like the Star of India Sapphire or Elizabeth Taylor's 69.5-carat diamond that was renamed the Taylor-Burton diamond. Which is the main reason I bought my wife a ring I knew she wouldn't want, and would hardly ever wear. I wanted to give her a gift with a *name*. Now why would any sane man do that? It actually reminds me of knowledge gleaned from research that our ad agency conducted when we handled the Van Cleef & Arpels account a few years back.

It seems that men and women buy—and give—jewelry for entirely different reasons. Just because a woman is wearing a ruby brooch or a necklace with a diamond the size of an acorn doesn't mean she actually likes it. She *might* have liked it if her husband remembered what she actually preferred, i.e., a canary diamond versus a ruby, a bracelet versus the brooch, or something daintier rather than a glittering neck brace. But then, you don't know her husband!

The husband bought the piece to a) flatter his ego, b) tell the world he's important and has made it, and c) couldn't care less what his wife likes. He thinks she's damn lucky to be getting anything after all these years; she's not twenty and what's he getting these days, anyway? So there you have it. The reasons men buy women expensive jewelry and the resentment women have to wearing it. Unless, of course, like Ellen Barkin, they sell it post-divoirce for a major haul! So, I decided that after twenty-two years of building and then selling one of the most successful advertising agencies in America, my wife was going to have a ring with a name. I pondered the Earn-Out Emerald or just plain Earn Out. I thought it has a nice ring to it, excuse my pun.

So once the final payment hit the account and I suddenly became one of the youngest chairmen in America (read: hood ornament), I did a little shopping for my ego. And you know what? It felt good to be able to do it. Because every time my wife wears the Earn Out (to match the emerald and diamond earrings I bought her . . . which she also doesn't wear), I know that every glimmer and glint will make up for every ass I had to kiss, every line of copy I had to change for some boorish client, every credit someone else took for my creative idea, and the looks of every Wall Street guy who asked me if people in the ad business actually make a *real* living. That during this economic downturn, I had earned the right to a little vulgarity.

You might be wondering what my wife, Dana, said when I tell you that I gave her the Earn Out anyway. I am not lying when I tell you she cleaned the hummus off the setting, trying the ring on her long slender finger, and looked at it like it was an alien. Then she actually looked me straight on, her green eyes glittering like the stone. "You know I don't like jewelry. It doesn't interest me. But, Richard, if you were going to do it, couldn't it have been just a *little* bit bigger?" she joked. Which just goes to show that nothing's ever "too" big. Having worked over the last two decades for some of the biggest names in the business world, I know they didn't get to where they were because they thought small or in half carats. Big dreams, big aspirations, and big ideas lead to breakthroughs. Modesty and understatement can be wonderful virtues in a number of settings, but they don't often lead to fresh and vibrant thinking. One exercise I often use with clients is to create the future "big story" in the *New York Times* or *Wall Street Journal* and postdate it. Very often if you can dream it, it's the first step to getting there.

Just last week when I had my lunch with the kids from the George Jackson Academy, one of the fourth graders, named David Febrillet, told me he wanted to be a lawyer when he grew up. Then he added, so he could become president of the United States (and possibly the first Hispanic president). I loved that he was thinking so big at his age and encouraged him to continue to do so. David, please know I'll help you with your campaign when you're ready. You have my vote!

In the business world, it's ironic that creative people are often maligned or misunderstood. Yet creativity and big ideas start, shape, and move markets very often more than the numbers—one of the most famous iconic ads of the 1960s was DDB's Volkswagen ad, "Think small." It was in its day a big idea to feature and embrace a small auto. Breakthrough ideas always confront and go against mainstream thinking and the grain. If there's one thing that the ad business has taught me, it's that you have to think it to be it. I always tell that to young people starting out who come to see me for advice, when they are unsure about their career direction. I tell them, when it comes to work, it's just as important to know what you *don't want to do* as it is to know what it is you *do want to do*. In advertising, you need to end up truly feeling that you and what you do are one. The best way to do that is to try your hand at many things you think you might like at the beginning of your career and then narrow down the funnel.

My first real job (at age nine) was walking my neighbor Mrs. Greenhut's poodle. Perhaps I got paid a dollar or two a week walking Pookie (or whatever the dog's name was). In between go-cart rides and bike rides, I thought I was banking major coin. Clearly two dollars a week wasn't going to get me a house in "The Harbor," but it kept me in Fribbles. I also had a few summer internships that were fairly memorable and helped me understand what I *didn't* want to do. I graduated from dog walker to waiter at the Café Natural in Hewlett (where I was harassed by various, often demanding Five-Towns cougars). My favorite request was by a menopausal blonde in leopard print who actually sent back the water. "I didn't order it with ice [prononounced "oyce"]," she said as she leered at me. I was going to say something snide, but she did pinch my ass and then gave me a twenty-dollar tip, which was like hitting the lottery in 1979. I was both scrawny and naïve and too busy lusting after my high school girlfriend Sari-Ann (she of the voluptuous brassiere size) to care. Sari-Ann (hi, darling!) went to Hewlett High School, and I went to Lynbrook, and her strawberry blonde hair and green eyes (and gorgeous rack) had me at "hello"!

My first real summer job (through an ad in *WWD*) is a bit of a blur, but I filed papers in the accounting department on Seventh Avenue for Perry Ellis. It wasn't all that interesting until I was nabbed by Perry himself while I was leafing through the sample rack.

"Can I help you?" he smirked.

"I just had my eye on this jacket." It was a stripped red-and-blue blazer. "I have a date."

"With who?"

"My girlfriend."

"Really? Well, you can take it."

"Really?"

"Sure, try it on."

Now I wasn't going to turn down a free Perry Ellis blazer from Perry Ellis (as long as there were no strings attached). To his credit, he and a seamstress actually tailored the blazer on site for me. As he was on his knees with the seamstress (a bit weird for some kid with just a temp position), I decided to ask him a question that had been on my mind all summer.

"So, Perry, after working here all summer I have a question," I figured I'd ask.

"Go ahead," he said with pins in his mouth.

"Why is it you wear the same thing every day?" (A preppy blue shirt and khaki trousers.)

"I only wear this and have no patience for anything else. I design for people like you."

I respected Perry Ellis all the more for his honesty and his wardrobe of exclusively powder blue button-downs and khakis, but in the end, I knew fashion wasn't a career for me. I just didn't get a kick out of the clothes and walking into the office everyday. As I've gotten older, I have even gone more to Perry's way of thinking, buying multiple things I like, because who has the patience?

The next summer, my wonderful uncle and aunt (Chester and Paulette) pulled some strings to get me an internship at NBC. (I've always been against nepotism but was too young to fight it.) I was to work as an intern for the *Today* show in New York and Detroit for the 1980 Republican and Democratic conventions. It was a plum internship, and I was the only "non-talent" intern progeny. When everyone asked who *my* father was, I replied, "I was the illegitimate son of one of the executives." They believed me. I felt like a big shot delivering mail to Jane Pauley at 30 Rock, yet was dismayed when in Detroit we were put up in a motel in Dearborn, Michigan (next to a Bob's Big Boy). It was so dreary, and we were bused into the Renaissance Center for the Republican Convention. I had interest neither in politics nor the news and couldn't wait to get back to AB (Atlantic Beach) for the tuna salad and tanning. Clearly, I was *not* a newsman and had no interest in being the next Tom Brokaw. Also, they didn't have halibut salad in Dearborn. Who knew?!

So . . . I heeded my own advice and ruled out dog walking, waiting on tables, fashion, and the news. And then, one day, it came to me.

I was a bit dismayed that after two fairly illuminating summer experiences I hadn't found my path, and it definitely weighed on me as my friends were preparing themselves for pre-law or -medicine. I would like to say it was a vision or it was something weighty, but alas I cannot lie. My life was actually changed by Brandpa's TV. That's right, by one of the Sony Trinitrons Brandpa had sent up from Florida. I had been watching

TV and became overwhelmed by *Bewitched*. (Don't look at me that way! I mean, who was hotter than Samantha?) So what if everyone wanted to be Jonas Salk or Perry Mason?! At the end of the day (while I couldn't manage an advertising internship), I just knew that I would get a kick out of being Darrin Stephens and working at McMahon and Tate! My conversation with Marilyn (a.k.a. Maude) went something like this.

"Well, you look like the cat who swallowed the canary."

"I've got great news. I think I've decided I know what I want to do!"

"And that is?"

"I want to be Darrin Stephens."

"And who's that?"

"You know, the ad guy on *Bewitched*."

"Well, I want to be Dinah Shore, but I don't think Burt Reynolds is coming around."

"I think I want to go into advertising."

"Because you saw it on TV?"

"No, because I think it would be fun and creative."

To Marilyn's (a.k.a. Maude's) credit, she agreed. "I think that's a good idea. You could come up with all those catchy slogans. And maybe you'll meet Dinah. She's Jewish you know."

"Who?"

"Dinah Shore. She's a nice Jewish girl from the South. Very active in Hadassah!"

So there you have it. I went into the ad business because Dinah Shore did a Hadassah fundraiser! Now, Darrin may have been a bumbling adman, but he *was* still married to a hot little number, lived in a swell suburban house (which kind of reminded me of my house), wore cool suits, had a decent office, and came up with fun lines and presented off of storyboards. And I didn't need to go to Harvard or University of Pennsylvania (and guess what? I wasn't getting in) to do it. Yes, Darrin Stephens seemed like the perfect role model. He wasn't athletic and he had fun at the office. I wasn't serious or brooding like Dr. Kildaire, I didn't ponder like F. Lee Bailey, and while I had a shag and my mother wore pantsuits, we weren't musical like the Partridge Family. While I also agreed with Eva Gabor's sentiment, "Darling, I love you, but give me Park Avenue," I wasn't a Wall Street guy like Eddie Arnold and had no interest in having a pet pig. Darrin Stephens was the man! An adman! And so that's what I would be. (Also if you lined up Dana *and* my mother-in-law, Marcia, *and* Samantha *and* Endora—it wouldn't be so far from the truth. And it might be the reason I run out of the room when Dana does that little thing with her nose.) I'm just glad I had the good sense to pick *Bewitched*! I could have easily become a GO at Club Med, as my second favorite show on TV was *Gilligan's Island*. Samantha or Ginger? It's still a pretty hard toss-up. But no matter, all of Brandpa's Trinitrons seemed to have paid off.

My journey from adboy to adman has only happened because I was never limited by limited thoughts (that never occurred to me in the first place). Am I a Mad Man? Well, I'm not mad in the angry sense of the word. But I've come to embrace the madness of creativity as a real, big tool in business. It may be elusive and magical, hard to understand or pin down, but it's equally as important as bricks and mortar. In fact, advertising has become more than a culture of popularity; it is now the indicator of popular culture. And I am grateful to be part of it. While the only thing you can expect in life (and the ad biz) is change (thanks, Mom), I am truly excited by all the possibilities that the new media age and technology have brought the industry. Every day, I jump out of bed ready to embrace all the unbelievable new projects, including all the innovative projects at kbsp and my Nuestudio. But that, my friends, is a whole other story . . .

IMAGE GALLERY

Madboy in the style of Horst. Freud would have a field day with this photo.

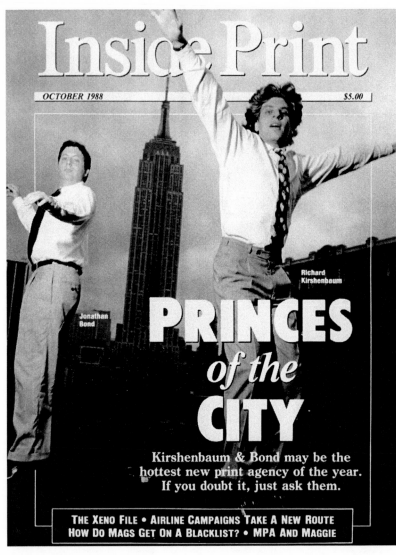

Inside Print

OCTOBER 1988 $5.00

Richard Kirshenbaum

Jonathan Bond

PRINCES
of the
CITY

Kirshenbaum & Bond may be the
hottest new print agency of the year.
If you doubt it, just ask them.

THE XENO FILE • AIRLINE CAMPAIGNS TAKE A NEW ROUTE
HOW DO MAGS GET ON A BLACKLIST? • MPA AND MAGGIE

I never denied being a prince

My press photo when I really was an adboy.
Everyone needs a cheesecake photo!

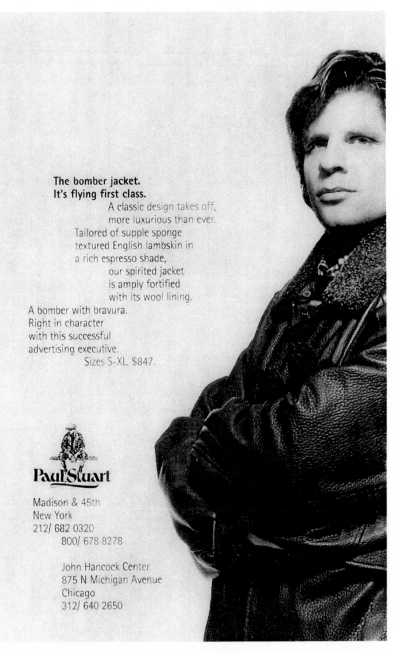

**The bomber jacket.
It's flying first class.**

A classic design takes off,
more luxurious than ever.
Tailored of supple sponge
textured English lambskin in
a rich espresso shade,
our spirited jacket
is amply fortified
with its wool lining.
A bomber with bravura.
Right in character
with this successful
advertising executive.
Sizes S-XL. $847.

Paul Stuart

Madison & 45th
New York
212/ 682 0320
     800/ 678 8278

John Hancock Center
875 N Michigan Avenue
Chicago
312/ 640 2650

It's nice to create ads. It's also nice to be in them!

Is Advertising Finally Dead?

Will legendary adman George (I want my MTV) Lois,
upstart Richard (No Excuses) Kirshenbaum, and their
chubby buddy be zapped into interactive oblivion?
First, a word from our sponsor...

$4.95 / Canada 5.95

Me and the Pillsbury Doughboy. Does it get any better?

223

It's big business

Me and Dana

SPECIAL THANKS

Dana, you will always be my everything and more. Words cannot describe how much I love, respect, and admire you and how lucky I am. Lucas, Talia, and Georgia, a father could not be prouder of his wonderful, smart children. To my fab sister Susan and Rob Perry, here's to always keeping the laughter going. To my in-laws Marcia, Fred, and Cookie Geier: You're the very best. To Aunt Paulette and Uncle Chester; the Kirschenbaum's with a "c;" Bonnie, Ilene, and Joel Joachim, Bryan and Marisa, here's to a great family. To Aunt Jackie and Armand Kalajian—all my love!

To the four brothers I never had but now have and their great spouses: David Mitchell and Jamie, Jordan Schur and Stephanie, Bippy Siegal and Jackie and Marc Glimcher and Andrea. Jamie—you are my second wife—no bills, though! Mark E. Pollack: to our telephone brotherhood, long may it reign.

To my nearest and dearest sisters from another mother: Patty Stegman and Danny—"Happy Birzday." Marisa Acocella Marchetto and Silvano—the best friends and best food anywhere (hi, Violetta and Tony!). Muffie Potter Aston and Dr. Sherrell Aston, you may have been born to the purple but you're true blue! Lisa Mirchin, the greatest wit, Wendy Kaufman and Steven Harkins, Lorinda Ash, Adriana Trigiani (now there's an author!) and Tim Stephenson, Ali Schneider and Jack, and Susan Krakower—I am so proud of you. To my assistant of 17 years, Carol O'Connell, and Ran who but who is better??? Thanks for everything!

Jon and Rebecca Bond. Jon a great business partner and friend of 24 years—it *was* fun, wasn't it?

To my G-dfather in the ad biz, the original Mad Man, Jerry Della Femina (I kiss the ring), and to his gorgeous wife, Judy Licht, thanks for all the years of love, advice, and friendship. To my big brother in the ad biz Donny Deutsch—I am truly grateful. To Lois Korey and Allen Kay for giving me my start. To Rocco and Ruth Campanelli for being such great mentors in every aspect of life. To James Patterson, Sue Read all a big thank you. To my consigliere David Wiener and Sheila—the very best there is!

To the late, great Jan Mitchell and Richard Siegal. You both taught me so much about generosity and "living large."

Thank you to Lori Greenberg and Alan Blum, as well as to Jill Weingarten, Nancy Temkin, and all the gals at Greenberg Kirshenbaum, who are the best in the biz.

Special thanks to my mentor and partner—truly the world's most interesting man, Chris Blackwell, Thank you, too, Meg Friedman and Lisa Gabor.

Thank you in no particular order to all the great people who make and have made life fun on a daily basis: Ron and Stephanie Kramer (Kramer style rules); my younger bro Jason Rosenfeld and Allie (rock on); the fabulous Phyllis George; Governor John Y. Brown; Morgan Spurlock; Robert and Serena Perlman; Joseph Klinkov; David Lauren and Lauren Bush; Tim and Saffron Case; Kenny and Shoshana Dichter; Lorre Erlick; Richard and Lisa Frisch; Harlan and Debbie Peltz; Gail Siegal; Stephen and Ilene Sands; Stephen and Leah Swarzman; Darius and Jill Bikoff; Larry and Joan Altman; Alan and Karen Wilzig; Zach Kutsher; Sara Rotman; Jason and Haley Binn; James Blank; Bob and Clara Lessin; Jeff and Amy Hock; Sachin and Babi Ahluwalia; Emanuele and Joanna Della Valle; Stephen and Stephanie Gottlieb; Jennifer Miller and Mark Ehret; Stefani Greenfield and Mitchell Silverman; Mort Zuckerman; and Rabbi Adam and Sharon Mintz.

To Debi Deutsch and Peter Drakoulias at TORCH, and my dear friend Alison Fahey. To all the good you do!

To my Open Road family: Jane Friedman, the doyenne of the publishing field and pioneer in e-publishing, thank you for everything. You really made it happen. To Jeff Sharp—you are incredible. To the Open Road team, Brendan Cahill, Luke Parker Bowles, Andrea Colvin, Greg Gordon, Mary McAvaney, Galen Glaze, Annie Jefferson, and Danny Monico. To Liz Anklow and Sean Cassidy, the uber-publicists at Dan Klores Communications—thanks for everything; you are the very best. I am privileged to work with Sandi Mendelson—thank you. To the very best editor in the business, Laura Yorke: You made it "all good." Thank you, Carol Mann, for your advice and vision. My dear friend Alex Drosin, thanks for all the matchmaking. Thanks to Eric Raymen, Rick Kurnit, and Jamie Wolfe for all the lawyering.

To Miles and Kelly Nadal and Lori Senecal: Thanks for your vision and support. And to all the kbp crew who are too talented and too numerous to count; I am grateful to each and every one of you for making it happen. And to our first kbp employee Julie Paciulli.

To some of my dearest friends and clients over the years: Clint Rodenberg; Penn Kavanagh; Bill Gentner; Lew Frankfort; Valerie Salembier; Stephanie George; Liz Nickles; Kenneth Cole; Courtney Clarke; Neil Cole; Dari Marder; John Pellegrine; Henri Barguardjian; Kenny Dichter; Gilles Hennessy; Mitchell Etess; Brad Jakeman; Anne MacDonald; Bernard Peillon; and Isabella Decitre. Thanks to Arnie Greenberg, Lennie Marsh, and Hyman Golden, as well as Tom Lee. Lewis Topper, Dave Karem and Joe Turner.

To the next generation of talent, Miles Skinner at The Nuestudio and Chad Jackson and Harry "Bee" Bernstein at The 88. To the new design mafia, Rafael de Cárdenas, Ryan Fitzgerald. I love you all! Here's to the future....

And last but not least, Ish "the Ish factor" Collins and for my tailors and shirtmakers in Naples, Sartoria Sabino and Salvatore Piccolo for always making me look fit and *expensive*.

copyright © 2011 Richard Kirshenbaum

cover design by Jim Tierney
interior design by Danielle Young

paperback: 978-1-4532-1144-1
hardcover: 978-1-4532-1962-1

Published in 2011 by Open Road Integrated Media
180 Varick Street
New York, NY 10014
www.openroadmedia.com

Follow Richard on Twitter and read his inspiring AD OF THE DAY: witticisms and pithy thoughts to live by

@rkirshenbaum

AD OF THE DAY: It's possible to think big—even about the small things.

AD OF THE DAY: Every once in a while you need to face the music—so you can write your own score.

AD OF THE DAY: Who you listen to is often more important than who you speak to.

AD OF THE DAY: A little bit of controversy keeps things interesting. Too much is a bore.

AD OF THE DAY: To quote my dad: "Either you're making money or losing money. There's no such thing as breaking even."

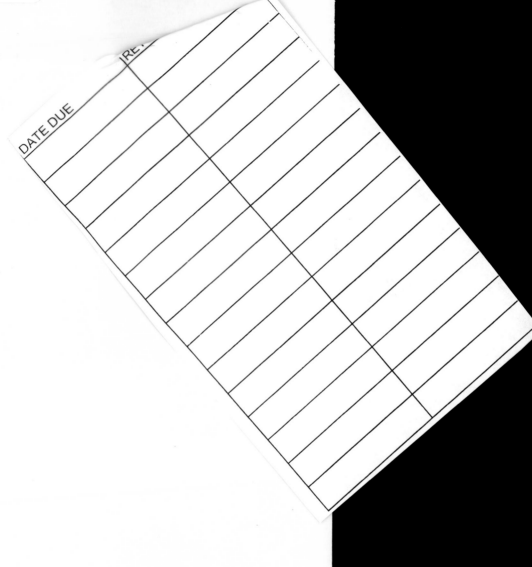

DATE DUE

CPSIA information can be obtained at www.ICGtesting.com
Printed in the USA
LVOW070442081211

258395LV00003B/13/P